GUIDANCE MONOGRAPH SERIES

SHELLEY C. STONE

BRUCE SHERTZER

Editors

GUIDANCE MONOGRAPH SERIES

The general purpose of Houghton Mifflin's Guidance Monograph Series is to provide high quality coverage of topics which are of abiding importance in contemporary counseling and guidance practice. In a rapidly expanding field of endeavor, change and innovation are inevitably present. A trend accompanying such growth is greater and greater specialization. Specialization results in an increased demand for materials which reflect current modifications in guidance practice while simultaneously treating the field in greater depth and detail than commonly found in textbooks and brief journal articles.

The list of eminent contributors to this series assures the reader expert treatment of the areas covered. The monographs are designed for consumers with varying familiarity to the counseling and guidance field. The editors believe that the series will be useful to experienced practitioners as well as beginning students. While these groups may use the monographs with somewhat different goals in mind, both will benefit from the treatment given to content areas.

The content areas treated have been selected because of specific criteria. Among them are timeliness, practicality, and persistency of the issues involved. Above all, the editors have attempted to select topics which are of major substantive concern to counseling and guidance personnel.

Shelley C. Stone

Bruce Shertzer

INDIAN
STUDENTS
AND
GUIDANCE

JOHN F. BRYDE
UNIVERSITY OF SOUTH DAKOTA

HOUGHTON MIFFLIN COMPANY · BOSTON
NEW YORK · ATLANTA · GENEVA, ILL. · DALLAS · PALO ALTO

Library of Congress Catalog Card
Number: 76–150391

ISBN: 0–395–12435–2

CONTENTS

EDITORS' INTRODUCTION

The author of this monograph has spent twenty-four years not, as he puts it, working with the Indian people but learning from them.

In the early days of the development of guidance and counseling Dr. Bryde felt his way in counseling Indian students, utilizing the emerging body of knowledge in that field and developing methods of his own that were more suited to the needs of the Indian student. In this monograph he shares some insights gained over these years spent as a counselor, teacher and administrator of Indian students. Dr. Bryde speaks the Sioux language fluently and is an adopted member of the Dakota or Sioux people with the Indian name of White Shield.

The author's experience with and knowledge of Indian people has enabled him to produce a thoroughly realistic and informative document having much inherent worth to anyone interested in working with the American Indian. Dr. Bryde's emphasis on Indian values and their relationship to that of the dominant American value system is basic to understanding the personality and behavior of the Indian in American society.

SHELLEY C. STONE

BRUCE SHERTZER

AUTHOR'S INTRODUCTION

One of the general functions of a counselor is to assist others in arriving at a happy response pattern to their total environment. Although each individual will have his own particular response to specific situations, his overall reaction to the most important areas of the environment will have been determined long before he is born by his forefathers; the moment he is born, the general response pattern of his culture begins to shape his behavior.

The Indian people, over many thousands of years, have adaptively worked out a response pattern to the total environment which they consider successful and which satisfies them. In order to understand his Indian client, the counselor of Indian students must have a thorough and appreciative knowledge of this Indian response pattern, also known as the Indian value system, which has shaped and produced his Indian client. Not only must a counselor understand the value system of his Indian client, but he must be aware of his own value system in order to avoid imposing it needlessly and perhaps harmfully on the Indian student.

This small volume seeks to assist the counselor of Indian students to understand his Indian client by presenting the positive Indian values that generate modern Indian behavior. The monograph also identifies variables that negatively influence the behavior of Indian students and thereby block their full development. Specific areas of cultural conflict are identified, and ways and means of resolving the conflict are explored. Indian personality is outlined and factors making for Indian motivation are presented. Methods for relating better to Indian clients, suggested by Indian students themselves, are also offered.

The writer has worked with thousands of Indian people from Canada to the borders of Mexico who have kindly shared their knowledge of the Indian value system. Therefore, despite individual tribal differences, most of the basic Indian values described here will apply to most Indian students.

JOHN F. BRYDE

A Preliminary Comment

One might legitimately ask from the start, what is so different about counseling an Indian? Why the special treatment? After all, a qualified counselor knows basic psychology, the ordinary human problems and their solutions, the various occupational goals that most people have, and he knows how to assist a student in availing himself of the means to achieve these goals.

One quick and practical answer to this is that many a counselor, often with advanced degrees and accomplished in all the skills of his profession, has been completely stumped in his initial and continuing face-to-face counseling sessions with Indian students. It quickly dawns upon such a counselor that there is something different about Indian students and that many of the ordinary counseling techniques that work so well with most students do not work at all with Indian students.

In pondering the answer to what is so different about the Indian student, one might well recall the ancient injunction of Socrates to teachers, "Before you teach, know your human subject." If one thinks that this is easy in regard to his Indian human subject, he should recall the words of James Fenimore Cooper: "Who shall fathom the mind of the noble red man?" In short, what teacher or counselor of Indian students really knows his Indian subjects? What training, study, or experience has he had to understand and appreciate the culture that has produced the Indian student? The answer is that the average counselor of Indian students has had very little study in Indian culture and is only faintly acquainted with the great psycho-socio-historical forces extending back over 20,000 years that have shaped modern Indian behavior.

One of the main reasons that teachers and counselors of Indian students know little about their human subjects is that the school system itself has completely ignored the Indian culture and value system. School systems have operated on the assumption that there is nothing worthwhile in the Indian culture to teach or to know, that the Indian youngster coming into kindergarten or the first grade is culturally an empty jar, and that the main function of the school is to fill this jar with all the treats of the white world.

By ignoring the Indian culture, or treating the Indian as though he had no culture, the school system has also ignored the only psychologically feasible way of motivating the Indian student, namely, by his value system. Social scientists have known for some years that the system of rewards and punishments (values) of one culture do not necessarily motivate people of other cultures. Yet, the American school system has used a non-Indian system of rewards and punishments, that is, non-Indian values, to motivate Indians. Despite the efforts of thousands of teachers and the expenditure of millions of dollars, the Indian has not changed. Change takes place in response to a felt need to change. The fact that the Indian has not changed indicates that he sees nothing in the non-Indian value system presented to him in the schools that creates in him a need to change.

In the whole history of Indian education one fact emerges with startling clarity: Very little effort has been made to really understand the Indian. The *American Heritage Book of Indians* (Josephy, 1961) has this astonishing statement:

> One thing is obvious: if the American Indians can claim direct descent from those early people of 15,000 to 20,000 years ago, and some undoubtedly can, then they are by far the oldest known race on earth. There is no evidence of the identifiable appearance of any of the other modern races, Mongolian, White or Negro, until much later.

The implication of this remark is something much more profound than surprise and admiration at this miracle of adaptive behavior in the act of mere physical survival. At its most significant level, it means these people have worked out adaptive responses to the most important part of the total environment, namely, to one another or to the human area. A successful culture should be judged not by how well it conquered the physical environment or in what it produced materially, but in how it solved the most vexing of all human problems, the problem of human relations. After all, man's major problems do not come from the physical environment alone but from other people. The Indian people, over a much longer span of time than that of the Western-European-American people, have developed a way of responding to and interacting with other people that suits *them*, and they are not about to change that mode of behavior. To the Indian, the white man is a relative newcomer to his human scene and many of his modes of behavior are bizarre, jarring, and unacceptable.

When counseling an Indian student, the counselor may unwittingly assume that the student accepts all the values of the dominant culture. But the student, convinced that his way of life is best, will listen to the counselor, taking in only what he perceives will help him become a better Indian and filtering out any suggestions or innuendoes unconsciously designed to make him into a white man. Nothing makes the average Indian angrier than his perception of the white's use of the words "integration", "assimilation", or "acculturation". Whatever meaning the white puts on these words, the average Indian interprets them as attempts to force him to become non-Indian. Indians, of course, do not wish to reject that which they are.

A skillful counselor, therefore, should function to help the Indian student become what he wants to become while remaining Indian. He must realize that the Indian student will aspire to the same vocational goals as other students, but that the meaning the Indian student will find in a vocational role and the type of human fulfillment he sees himself enjoying in it will very often be different from that of the non-Indian student. Suggesting non-Indian motives for seeking these vocational goals may alienate the Indian student, sometimes to the point of making him retreat from his original intention of pursuing a vocational objective. In order to avoid this, the counselor must know the Indian value system and utilize it properly. He must also avoid unwittingly signalling the assumed superiority of his own value system, thereby alienating the Indian student (Hickerson, 1966).

No Indian today will deny that the Indian people need knowledge and skills from the non-Indian world in order to survive. Acquisition of this knowledge and these skills is through the school system. What the Indian objects to is that in acquiring these necessary skills he is subjected to non-Indian ways of acting and to non-Indian systems of motivation. In order to gain the least important things in life, the mere tools or skills for making a living, the Indian is compelled by the average school system to go against the grain of his traditions which have been handed down over thousands of years.

From his very first education course every teacher, administrator, and counselor has had drummed into him that one of the primary objectives of education is to meet the needs of the child. On examining the nature of these needs, however, one very important thing is overlooked, especially in cross-cultural education. Beyond the biological needs for food and shelter and the psychological needs for love and security which are common to all people of all cultures, all of the other needs of man are largely culturally-induced or learned needs. It is these cultural needs of the Indian students that are completely ignored and therefore unfulfilled in the majority of schools teaching Indian children. The cultural or learned needs of the non-Indian child are, more or less, met and fulfilled, and these same cultural needs are presumed of the Indian child. But the 60 per cent national dropout rate for Indian students invalidates this assumption.

By way of concluding these introductory remarks, it should be pointed out that the counselor of Indian students works under several handicaps, one of the greatest of which is that, in the eyes of the Indian, he is a transient. Especially on the reservations, the young Indian student quickly draws the conclusion that the white personnel are here today and gone tomorrow. He sees the public health doctors serving their two-year terms and moving on. Teachers move on to better opportunities and new ones take their places. Missionaries of all denominations, with a few exceptions, come and go. Volunteers come out to the reservation "to help" for a year or two and then are gone. The reaction of the Indian student, then, is to guard his heart and not get too attached to transients.

There is no desire here to suggest that this is insurmountable. Despite his transient nature in the eyes of the Indian student, the non-Indian counselor can reach his Indian clients provided that he sincerely loves and respects them. As Dr. Helen Red Bird points out in her lectures, the Indian will respond to anyone, of any race or culture, whom he perceives as really accepting him. Whether he truly values and respects his Indian students is something which only the counselor himself can answer. One can use all the sweet words in the world and flash constantly the pearliest of smiles, but if down deep he does not really respect and value his Indian students it will be perceived, and all his friendly efforts will be in vain. If he regards his Indian students as merely interesting sociological or anthropological specimens, the Indian students will tolerate him, but will not let him influence them (Vontress, 1968).

Another handicap under which the counselor in the typical Indian school labors is that by the time he receives him as a client in junior high school or later, the Indian student's personal development potential may have been severely damaged by his school experiences. He may be already scarred psychologically and much of the counselor's work will of necessity need to be therapeutic. What this often means is that at a time when most students are open to new experiences, the counselor must concentrate on removing the barriers to growth in the Indian student.

2

Indian Values

In this discussion of Indian values, it should be noted that a taxonomy and terminology of Indian values will vary among writers. It is the belief of this writer that most of the Indian values can be reduced to the values considered here. Despite the many differences among the Indian peoples in language, custom, and even physical appearance, there is a remarkable similarity in certain basic attitudes and values which most of them possess in varying degrees.

Good Advice from Indian Wisdom

The fundamental value from which most of the other Indian values flow is very ineptly termed "Good Advice from Indian Wisdom". When one asks old Indians, as the writer has done innumerable times over the years, "Who is the *good man* that everyone admires? What kind of a person is he?", he will not get an immediate response because an elderly Indian rarely answers an important question right away. He usually lowers his head and thinks, sometimes with his eyes closed. Finally, he will raise his head and say quietly, "The man that everyone admires is this: he can always give you good advice, and he will always help you if he can." When the people are in trouble and don't know what to do, they can always go to him and he will advise them rightly because he is wise." Again and again, this answer will come back in varying forms. On all reservations, scattered throughout the various districts there are these natural leaders of the people. They may not necessarily be the elected representatives on the various tribal councils. Yet, when a person is in trouble and needs advice and help, he will travel seventy to eighty miles to talk to such people. The old Indian may have patched clothes, may be using an upturned barrel for a chair and may not have seen a dollar bill in the last six months. Yet, it is to this type of a person that people go for advice, not to their tribal attorney or to their local missionary or to their banker or to a particularly brilliant teacher at the local school. They go to the Indian type of *good man* because he can give them something none of the others can give — good advice, flowing from his Indian wisdom.

A study of Indian wisdom reveals that all of reality is *one, related, holy, and God-permeated*. Things, including men, are judged by what they are inside, and not by what they appear to be or by what they have.

Everything is one. The oneness of everything is not the pantheism of one of the schools of the ancient Greeks because in this mysterious oneness each thing retains its individuality. The oneness of everything does not have to be explained in the logical terms of Western-European thought. It is just there. The universe with all its parts, including man, is a "one thing." As heirs of Aristotle, Western man has a compulsion to understand and explain to others in logical terms the phenomena he observes. The Indian also observes the natural phenomena. To the Indian, however, the important thing is to understand them to his own satisfaction. He does not have to explain or defend his understanding of them to the satisfaction of others, nor does he proselytize or take the initiative in teaching his findings. His method of arriving at his understanding is more intuitive and contemplative as he strives to grasp the essence of things.

In the account of the Indian writer named Black Elk, it is explained that the unity of all things was expressed in various symbols and rituals (Brown, 1953). One of the Indian's favorite designs, the circle, which is the perfect figure, expressed this unity. The *tipi*, while functionally round, also expressed the unity of all things (Neihardt, 1961). The seasons move in a great circle, as well as the winds that blow. Everything comes from the earth, lives out its existence, and returns to the earth to begin the great circle all over again. People dance in a circle and they sit in a circle, not only to see one another better, but to express their oneness. In smoking the pipe together, the individuals, represented by the grains of tobacco, become one in the smoke as it rises, and the smoke, representing their oneness, becomes one again with the universe. Just as the body has many individual parts all making up a whole entity, so all things in the universe are different parts making up a "one thing".

All things are related. Each thing that exists, no matter how different it might appear to be from another, is related. Mysterious "blood veins" connect everything in a bond of common relationship. Blood relationships are established by tracing people to common ancestors. Since everything on earth is traceable to a common ancestor, a common "mother" earth, then all things are related. The earth might produce a rock, a rabbit, a tree or a man. Since all these different things come from the same mother earth, then they are all related in some mysterious, mystical way. In spite of outward appearances, such as hardness, immobility, or insensitivity, the rock has a common relationship to the rabbit and the man within its essence and behind its exterior differences. A person should always strive to be aware of these relationships to all things and just as he strives to live on good terms with his blood relatives, so should he strive to live with awareness of all these harmonious relationships, animate and inanimate, around him.

Each thing that exists is holy or sacred. In Western culture a thing does not become holy or sacred in the religious sense until it is blessed, or consecrated and invested with sacredness by some religious rite. It is then set aside for special use on special occasions. The Indian, however, regards each and every thing that exists as having sacredness in much the same manner as the non-Indian does after imposing sacredness on the object from outside of it. Each and every thing that exists has its power or its holiness that is in it intrinsically. As such it is to be revered. While one object may be holier or more sacred than another, the power or sacredness already present emanates from within and is not imposed from without.

An object can exhibit its power and sacredness either actively, such as in the wind blowing or a large animal charging, or passively, such as in a large rock enduring. Whether one calls the power gravity or anything else, there is still a power in it that is peculiar to that object. By contemplating an object in nature — a tree, a flower or an eagle — it is possible for one to "get at" that power and share it. Thus, holiness in medicine men or holy men is something developed from within the person by contact with the various powers in surrounding objects.

The Indian believes that all existing things — rocks, animals, plants — talk to one another and emanate their powers. If one meditated long enough he could hear this talking, learn from these objects, and share in these emanations of power. Man's constant intellectual thrust, then, is to get inside things and perceive them as they are and not to be deterred by mere external appearances of the invisible *real* world.

Black Elk said, "We are walking in a world of darkness but we will soon come to a world of light." The type of knowledge appreciated by the Indian mind, then, is that based upon understanding the hidden world around him. The way to develop this understanding is to try always to perceive things as they are internally and not as they externally appear to be or by properties they might have.

The constant effort to get at the essences of things puts the Indian in contact with a world largely invisible to most other men. It is this awareness of the sacredness of each and every thing that makes the Indian ever alert to the essence of each thing, including each and every man, and in his constant search for this inner contact, he is undeterred by external appearances. This attitude, of course, has profound implications for the school system because models of human success and norms for judging people offered in the typical school system are at odds with the Indian model of human success.

The Indian believes that God is everywhere and in everything. When a non-Indian comes to live among the Indian people, one of the very first things that impresses him is the Indians' constant, familiar and reverent use of and reference to the name of God. They speak of God as a third person present in the conversation, which, to their way of thinking and due to their level of awareness, He is. In such frequent and spontaneous references to God they will use sweeping gestures to indicate His presence everywhere, or point upwards usually raising their eyes as well. This appreciative awareness of and constant spontaneous response to God is refreshing to the non-Indian whose own awareness of God is too often obscured and made intermittent by the pursuit of material things and by his conditioning to respond to God at scheduled times.

Although they do not have a refined theology, the Indian people know that in some mysterious way God is responsible for their existence, that He takes care of them, is personal to them, has mercy on them, and will respond to prayers sincerely made. The Navajos have a belief that wherever they go, God is behind them, above them, below them, in front of them and in them. To walk in awareness of and in harmony with this reality is to walk in beauty.

In the old times the Indian people never undertook any activity, large or small, without praying first. They prayed upon rising in the morning; they prayed before eating — *wosnapi* the Sioux called it, dropping or spilling a small amount of food on the ground, returning it to the earth in thanksgiving for it. They prayed before hunting, before going on the warpath, and on returning from both. They prayed when friends or strangers visited and smoked the pipe with them. After winning his war with the U.S. government, Red Cloud gave a speech at the famous Cooper Union in New York. Thousands crammed the great hall to see and hear this famous "savage" fresh from the plains. They were stunned as he opened his speech with a long and fervent prayer for peace. Sitting Bull revealed the attitude common in all the great chiefs when he said that one of the most important duties of a chief was to pray for his people every day.

This awareness of God and their natural response to Him is very much alive in the Indian people today. It is a common practice at gatherings, whether an anniversary feast or a P.T.A. meeting, to call upon any layman present to lead them in prayer. Without any hesitation or embarrassment, the one called upon will rise and pray spontaneously from his heart. To this day, if one rises early enough on the reservations, he can hear the soft drums and prayer chants of Indians as they greet the dawn — frequently coming from people that the local missionary has almost despaired of getting into a church to respond to God for a scheduled service on Sunday. Medicine men and Indian holy men who have never spent a day in a seminary pray with a fervor and spontaneity that would gladden the heart of a missionary.

With a world view, then, that sees everything as one, related and holy, with God everywhere and in everything, the Indian is otherworldly in that he responds to levels of reality largely hidden from the non-Indian's eyes. This makes for profound differences in the manner in which the Indian perceives and reacts to other people as well as in his models of human success. What the Indian looks for and admires in a person is his inner qualities judged by Indian standards: Is he filled with wisdom (enabling him to give good advice), and is he generous and helpful? These are some of the greatest of the Indian values.

Implications

Values, for the most part, until examined, are practiced and transmitted unconsciously, frequently by non-verbal cues. The tone of the voice, a gesture, an innuendo, a laugh are frequently the unconscious means to convey an attitude toward what is to be admired or disapproved. Success in the dominant American culture is often measured by material achievement. The model of success or the type of person to be admired is determined by what he has and not necessarily by what he is inside. A youngster may learn to admire this type of success largely by non-verbal cues from his parents. For instance, the family could be riding in a car when they might pass the large, expensive house of a wealthy man. The father might say, "Look at that house. I'll bet that cost him over a hundred thousand. He must be worth a couple million." The child might not know the difference between one dollar and one dime, but what he does get is the tone of admiration in the father's voice as he speculates about the other man's worth according to a financial standard. Such a child is already unconsciously learning an important value in his culture. As he grows up, he is bombarded by additional cues, verbal and non-verbal, from television, movies, magazines, books, and school that fairly soak him in the principle that the truly successful person is the affluent one. He learns, in effect, that this is the type of person that every sensible individual should strive to be.

The Indian youngster likewise gets his cues, verbal and non-verbal, concerning modes of activities and types of persons to be admired. In regard to the same situation, parents from different cultures will communicate to their children their own perceptions of approval or disapproval — or amusement. Using the same example as above, the Indian youngster could get from his parents a completely different set of cues. His father might look at the house and say in Indian, "He must be *really* rich." The hidden cue that the Indian youngster gets, however, is the chuckle in the father's voice which dismisses the display of wealth as frivolous. As he grows up, the Indian youngster continues to receive these non-verbal and verbal cues of amusement at money-making behavior as the most important thing in life. At the same time, he is receiving positive cues as to the type of person that his parents and grandparents admire. They could be talking about an Indian wise man when the grandfather might say, "He is *really* a good man because he is wise and helps you out." The cue that the Indian youngster would get would be a tone of admiration or a positive gesture that the grandfather would unconsciously use as he praised this type of person.

Every summer, the tourists roll through the reservations by the thousands. They frequently pull their big cars up in front of a general store and step out exuding an air of confidence and affluence. Spotting a couple of old-time Indians sitting in front of the store, they will make polite conversation about the weather or some light topic for a while, then ask the old-timers if they would mind having their pictures taken. After the pictures, they will slip the old-timers a half dollar and drive off, delighted at getting a picture of such quaint old people with their long braids, different clothes and big, odd-shaped hats. What they do not know is that, while they found the oldtimers quaint and amusing, the old-timers were chuckling softly to one another, even more amused at them because they so obviously considered the pursuit of money, seen in their expensive car and clothes, as the most important thing in life. This Indian attitude toward wealth is being signalled to Indian young people today and counselors should be aware of this when dealing with Indian students. An Indian adolescent will want to earn money to make a decent living but will not have the attitude that this is the most important thing in life.

What is most pertinent here is to note that, to the Indian way of thinking, one does not have to go to school in order to become the type of person, the model of success, that the Indian admires. One becomes this type of success not through school but simply by living rightly, by observing, thinking, and praying. The schools, of course, can offer skills to keep one alive as he strives for true, Indian-like success. The kind of knowledge that Indians respect usually goes with old age. Old people are respected not only because they have lived a long time but also because they have wisdom. Respect is shown to these wiser, older people by listening to and following their advice. It is interesting to note that in the Sioux language, the word for old man is *wicahcala*. Etymologically, this is the intensive of *wicasa*, "man", and therefore means "really a man" or a "real man." Since the old man's strength and youthful handsomeness are gone, the real manliness, the apex of masculinity that makes him "really a man" is his knowledge and wisdom which are the true qualities that the Indian people admire most in a man. Similarly, the Sioux word for old woman is *winunhcala,* which is the intensive for *winyan,* "woman", and means "really a woman" or a "real woman." Since her beauty and physical attractiveness are gone, the true womanly qualities that are really admired in a woman are her knowledge and wisdom.

The writer has heard elderly Indians solemnly tell persons around forty-five years of age, "You were born yesterday. You don't know anything yet." A typical Indian meeting is a long affair in which everyone has his say. At such meetings there will always be some elderly people listening patiently while the younger people speak. Finally, when the meeting has gone on for some time, an elderly person will slowly rise and say, "Listen to me. I am an old man," or "I am an old woman," and instantly there will be silence in the hall. Having given the highest credentials possible for authority to speak, the old person will proceed to deliver his views. It is expected that the younger people will show their respect by following the advice of the old people.

One should be aware that the above is not a dry, abstract description of a cultural system that existed in the past. The described values are basic, living attitudes toward ultimates that are vibrant and actively influencing the thinking of thousands of people today. Young Indian people who are the recipients of the largely unconscious cues signalling these attitudes may not be able to articulate or organize these values but the values are there, influencing their thought and behavior.

Adjustment to or Harmony with Nature

One of the sharpest differences between the Indian and the white man's attitudes toward the human part of the total environment is seen in the manner in which an Indian will address a gathering of people even when it is made up largely of strangers. Whereas the white will typically begin his address by greeting those present with the words, "Ladies and gentlemen," the Indian will begin by saying "My relatives," or "My brothers and sisters." The phrase "my relatives" is not just a polite form of address, but reflects a basic attitude toward people in that the Indian sees all people as related. Beyond strict blood relationships, all men have a deeper metaphysical relationship that makes everyone truly related. Toward all men, then, the Indian wants to act as relatives should act. Since all men are in one family, they should all work together, getting along with one another and helping one another out.

One of the most remarkable similarities among the Indian peoples is the quiet but firm mental set of getting along with others. The Indian has a built-in sensitivity and responsiveness to the feelings of others. In his social relationship with others, the Indian is a natural example of John Henry Newman's definition of a gentlemen as one who would not deliberately cause another pain. There is a gentleness, a quietness and unobtrusiveness in the Indian personality that compels him to get along with others. Many non-Indians label this as shyness; it contrasts with the competitiveness of the majority culture. Far from being shyness, the Indian's quiet, soft-spoken manner in dealing with people derives from his world view in which all men are related and should be treated as such.

In order to understand Indian behavior one cannot over-emphasize the necessity of realizing that the Indian, from his world view, is actively aware of himself as a living part of all of nature. Each part of total nature is active and alive and influences all of the other parts and consequently, the living whole. Since the active, living whole is greater than any active, living part, it is up to the individual to adjust himself to the whole. The offending or upsetting of one individual part could cause that offended part to upset another with a subsequent "domino" effect upon the whole. Hence, one must be sensitive to and adjust himself to each individual part so as not to disrupt the mysterious harmony of the total environment. Rather than adjust things (including people) to him, the Indian is aware that he, as the one responsible for keeping the balance among all things, must adjust himself to them.

This harmony and balance with nature, springing from his reverent awareness of being a part of a holy total, cautions the Indian to re-arrange nature just enough to get along. When it is cold, he rearranges it just enough to keep warm. When it is hot, he rearranges it just enough to keep cool. When he needs clothing or food, he rearranges it just enough to have a covering for his body and to remove his hunger. The more typical non-Indian attitude is to conquer nature as totally as possible. Nature is something unfeeling, to be used and exploited. Whereas men in the dominant culture often seek to control and dominate nature in order to determine their future, the Indian only seeks to control himself; it is from here that the harmony and balance of nature flows. Since the only time one can exercise this inner control in order to keep the balance is now, the emphasis on meaningful living is on the *now*.

It is almost common knowledge that historical incidents promote attitudes among a people which endure long after the experiences have passed. Among the Indian people the almost universal experience of living out their lives among relatives or the extended family gave rise to the attitude that everyone was related even if there were no immediately obvious blood lines. In the old days, Indian peoples lived in small groups, all of whom were related by blood, marriage, or adoption. When a child was born, whether in a *tipi, hogan,* or a cave, the members of his immediate family were not only those in his dwelling but all the people in the village. As the Indian child grew and structured his world, he did not call one woman "mother" ex-clusively. For instance, among the Sioux, all the sisters on his mother's side were called "mother" also. This was not just a term of courtesy but one endowing a true motherly function since they had all the responsibilities and privileges that the biological mother had. They trained the child, rewarded him, punished him, even nursed him if the occasion warranted it. In such circumstances, with so many mothers taking care of him, it could take several years for the child to sort out his biological mother. With two, three, or four mothers to love as he grew up, such a child had a greater sense of security and his emotions were more diffuse than a child whose whole security was bound up in one mother. The same held true for the child's father. His father's brothers were not called "uncle" but "father" and they had the privileges and responsibilities of the biological father. Consequently, if a child lost his biological parents, his sorrow was less keen than that of a child with just one mother and father.

A child also grew up with a large number of functional brothers and sisters besides his immediate biological family. For a male, all of the cousins on his father's side were called "brothers" or "sisters." For a female, all of the cousins on the mother's side were called "brothers" or "sisters". These brothers and sisters had the same relationship and responsibilities to the Indian child that real biological brothers and sisters had.

Among the Dakotas or Sioux, there are twelve different words for "cousin". The use of the proper term depends on whether the cousin is on the mother's or father's side, is male or female, younger or older and on whether it is a male or female speaking. Social scientists point out that an important value in a culture will usually have a rich vocabulary supporting it. The abundance of relationship terms among the Indian people indicates the importance of the value of harmony with nature. Traditional Indian people, in their dealings with others who were not strictly relatives, did not like to maintain relationships simply on a friendship basis. Since the proper way to relate with people was as relatives, they would adopt one another at various levels. Movies and TV are replete with scenes of Indians adopting whites as "blood brothers" or at other levels of relationship. To this day, traditional Indian people call one another, not by their proper names but by their relationship name.

Whether one chooses to explain it in terms of operant conditioning, classical Pavlovian conditioning or some other theory, one learns his behavior largely from the reactions of those closest to him. It is from his initial and continuing experiences within his kinship system that an Indian learns how to be peculiarly an Indian. It is within his kinship group that he receives all the verbal, non-verbal and unconsciously given cues to revere and adjust to nature in the total environment.

Generosity and Sharing

One does not have to live long among the Indian people today to realize that the Indian value of generosity or sharing is still very much alive and active. A third-grade boy will step up to the counter of the school store, put his coin down and point to the candy bar he wants. On receiving the candy bar, he automatically will break it in half and, hardly looking to identify the one standing next to him, will share half of the candy bar and go away contentedly chewing on his half. A high-school boy will spend his last coins in buying a pack of cigarettes, walk into a crowded recreation room, take one cigarette for himself and pass out the rest to the eager hands around him. Three minutes after he bought the cigarettes, he will toss the empty pack into the nearest waste basket. Another high-school boy will receive a new coat in the mail and wear it proudly to the next school dance. For the next three months the same coat will appear on cousins and friends at the weekly dances and it may be several months before the original owner wears his new coat again. Like the other Indian values, this particular value of generosity arose from a world view and from actual historical experiences in which sharing was necessary for survival.

The Indian people regard everything on the earth, the buffalo, deer, birds, grass, the trees in the forest, and the land as belonging to everyone. When one killed an animal for food, he was only the providential agent who brought the animal down and it still belonged to everyone even though it was now dead and in the hands of a particular hunter. Food such as berries, fruit, and vegetables, growing in the prairies and the forests belonged to everyone and waited only to be gathered. Private property, as it is known today, extended only to one's personal clothing, weapons, and medicine objects. The full dimensions of what this value really meant to the people is seen in the Dakota or Sioux word *woiyowaja*. Literally translated, this means a mutual right to one another's possessions, or "I have a right to what is yours if I need it and you have a right to what is mine if you need it."

As the Indian moved into his total environment, whether warring or hunting, he was always aware of his relatives and friends. Whatever he did he did for the group, which shared not only the game that was brought in but also the reputation of individual members. An Indian group often became strong and powerful because of one or two accomplished warriors or hunters. People from other groups would hear about the prosperity of a group caused by one or two brave members and would come and join the prosperous group making it, in turn, even stronger.

One of the reasons for the necessity of sharing and generosity, of course, was the very uncertainty of the hunt or the food-gathering process. Since one could never be sure that he would get something that day, he had to rely upon the generosity of his relatives or friends and they, in turn, had to rely upon him. Strength and security laid in the group. This made for a psychological security that is very difficult for a non-Indian even to imagine. This same sense of security still exists to a large degree among many of the Indian people. For instance, they will embark on relatively long journeys with very little money and supplies but with a confidence and peace of mind incomprehensible to the non-Indian. Such people know that they will get help along the way because they have experienced this before and because they themselves have helped others in similar circumstances.

The Indian today lives in two worlds, the Indian and the non-Indian. Within the security of his Indian world, surrounded by his relatives and friends, wherever he looks he sees faces turned toward him with hearts open to give and share whenever he needs something. Even though individually and collectively there is very little to share, the common attitude and mental set is there. One simply expects it.

Turning from the common, collective-sharing attitude of his Indian world and looking into the affluent non-Indian world, the traditional Indian is puzzled by what he regards as stinginess. Brought up to share whatever he had whenever there was a need, the traditional Indian's attitude is that, if he were affluent, he would share. Whatever the Indian receives from the non-Indian world, whether in the form of education, hospitalization, or welfare, he regards as only the right order of things. While he is grateful, it is not in the sense of receiving a gratuity but because other human beings are following the right order of doing things as he sees it.

In the old days there was unlimited giving because there was unlimited getting. One could always go out hunting or gathering and thus replenish his stock. Today, the giving is limited by the size of one's pay check, although the desire to share unlimitedly is still strong among traditional Indian people. This limitation on sharing brings about considerable tension between younger wage-earning Indian people and their older relatives. A young Indian couple just starting out, one or both with college degrees, may hold teaching or government office positions. However, like many young couples across the country, they are heavily in debt. They live in a neat, small house and drive a relatively new compact car. On pay day, after making time payments on their car and furniture, and purchasing groceries for the next two weeks, they may literally have only fifteen or twenty dollars in cash for incidentals. When an older relative comes around for financial help involving thirty or forty dollars, they are compelled to tell him that they simply do not have it. The older Indian, however, sees the nice house, the furniture, the new car, and the like, and to his way of thinking they are relatively rich. He is hurt when they turn him down because he feels that in some way they are not telling him the truth. The young people, in turn, are hurt because they really cannot help. Many young Indian people faced with this problem solve it by moving to other Indian areas where they do not have relatives, although this brings another problem of having to adjust to unfamiliar surroundings.

In making young Indian people aware of their values, they must also be made aware that, in the old days, there was priority among those with whom one shared: One shared first with his immediate family, then relatives, then friends. Any reversal of this order was a failure in responsibility toward others as sometimes occurs today when one will share with friends first (frequently drinking buddies), then share with the family that which is left over. A typical case is that of the man who gave a relative in need of money for an emergency almost his entire pay which he intended to use to satisfy some outstanding debts of his own. As a consequence of his reverse priority in sharing, he lost his car and TV and could get no futher credit at the grocery store. His family was in dire need for adequate food and clothing for the next two weeks and suffered considerably. An awareness of traditional priorities in sharing could help young Indian people today to make the proper adjustments.

In line with this, students could be shown the origin of their desire to share with others. They could also be shown that, due to the changed social situation in which they now live, although the same priorities (family, relatives, and friends) remain, there is a new ingredient in that which is shared, namely, savings in the bank. Different circumstances in which they now live make such savings a necessity for each family. Young Indians could be shown that the same priorities still exist and that once they put something out of each pay check in the bank, they could share with relatives and friends that which is left over. They thus could make conscious new applications of the old value. Lest one be carried away by expectations of such ideal behavior, it would be well to recall that there are vast numbers of non-Indians who live each month right to the limits of their salaries and who save only by reason of withholdings for social security and company retirement plans.

Also in line with bringing traditional behavior to consciousness is the necessity of making young Indian people aware of the other area of shared actions, that is, praise and shame. Traditionally, when one did something good, the whole group shared in the praise he received. One or two great hunters or warriors would attract other people to the group and the whole group rose together, assisting one another. A great chief was great only so long as he produced, and in producing he attracted others to the group. During the years of their greatness and for years afterwards, people would proudly say, "We are Red Cloud's people," or "We are Geronimo's people."

To this day, Indian people have an awareness of one another as members of their Indian group that is unsurpassed by any other group of people. An Indian will instantly feel a relationship with a strange Indian. When one Indian does something great the whole group rejoices in it and when one Indian does something bad the whole group feels it deeply. When Billy Mills won the 10,000 meter Olympics in Japan, not only did his own tribe, the Sioux, rejoice, but every Indian in the land pointed him out and said, "He's an Indian."

In practical terms young Indian students can be shown that when they do well in school, whether by giving a good answer in class or starring on the basketball team, the whole group profits. If (with the help of the schools) they were aware of traditional Indian behavior, they would realize that they were actually letting the group down by not doing their best. Instead of pulling down competent people, traditional Indian behavior requires that they be encouraged and supported, because the whole group shares their praise.

When one endeavors to analyze and compare objectively a system of living founded on individual competition such as in the dominant culture, and a system of cooperative living such as in the Indian culture, it is well to recall that in the former the losers far outnumber the winners; the tension of the competition more often than not results in bigger and better things, but not necessarily in better and happier people. The Indian system of cooperative living in which everyone gains and in which people are placed first and things second in its cooperative priorities would seem to provide valuable lessons for which the general society has need.

Individual Freedom

The Indian value of individual freedom derives from the Indian world view and from historical experience in which individual freedom was necessary for survival. The total purpose of the Indian's intellectual thrust into the environment was to produce understanding of the natural and human phenomena that confronted him, an understanding satisfying to the individual and one which he did not have to defend or explain to others. Since the source of this understanding was the person's mind, then the action and result of this precious quality was always respected for what it did for the individual and was never questioned. The fact that his knowledge satisfied him was all that mattered.

Since a person used his free will to follow his own conclusions to things, his judgments and subsequent actions were never questioned. An individual, even a child, came to his own decisions freely from within himself, utterly uncoerced from without. It was the responsibility of elders to set up the best possible stimuli in the form of advice to guide the individual to a wise decision, but in the guiding stimuli there was no coercion or threat of the "You do this or else!" nature.

Historical experiences reinforced the Indian's attitude that freedom was necessary for each and every individual. In the old days, one was relatively safe and protected by numbers in the confines of the village or the camp circle. The moment one stepped outside of this safety, however, he was surrounded by enemies and the harsher elements of the environment. He was on his own and no one could force him to make the right decisions to survive. Since outside the camp circle he had to stand upon his own two feet in order to survive, this practice was promoted within the protection of the group.

This lesson in individual freedom began from the moment that the child left his mother's lap. The child might crawl to a cactus and start to reach out to touch it. Right away, he would hear, "ssshhh . . . don't do that." He would look at his mother, then back at the tempting cactus. If he decided to touch the cactus, he would prick himself but not enough to injure himself seriously. He was not, however, pulled away from the cactus ahead of time; he was not coerced. Another time, he might be reaching for a small bug that could bite him but not seriously hurt him. Again, he would hear the "ssshhh . . . don't do that." Again, he would look from his mother to the bug and might or might not decide to touch the bug. At any rate, as the child grew, he quickly learned two things: he himself had to make the decision, and he had better listen to advice.

The child was never subjected to physical punishment. This would be a way of forcing one's will on another person and was never done. His greatest punishment was his own inner humiliation from mistakes made in not following advice, as well as from the ridicule of his peer group and from his elders. Since all of his life's activities were ordered to survival and self-fulfillment, he learned eventually to follow advice as the more important element of individual freedom. If he did not, then the worst of all possible consequences could follow, namely, loss of life. This is one of the reasons that old people were so respected. From their wisdom, they could give in their advice the guidelines for survival and self-fulfillment. Thus it was that the traditional, old-time Indian definition of the value of individual freedom was: following advice, you yourself decide to do the right thing to survive at the best level possible for you.

With the passing of warfare and hunting, younger people began to forget the necessity of following advice because the old consequences no longer prevailed. Younger people today are more aware of that part of the value by which they make their own decisions but have forgotten the most important part of the value, the following of advice. This hurts the elderly Indians because they see the younger people failing in an act that was of great importance — following the advice of their elders. As one elderly Indian put it recently in praising a younger man, "He's a good man. When you talk to him, he listens, all over."

Once an Indian student is aware of the expected Indian mode of behavior, the counselor is in an ideal position to help him. The counselor may inquire what his parents and grandparents have advised him to do, then suggest some possibilities without any element of coerciveness in it. The average Indian will listen to all of this, then put it together and make his own decision *from within*. This is one of the reasons why modern counseling techniques frequently do not work with Indian students. Much of modern counseling influenced by Carl Rogers expects the client to verbalize his feelings. Encouraged nondirectively by the counselor, the client solves his problems just by talking them out. An Indian, on the contrary, does not verbalize in an effort to solve his problems. More typically, an Indian will withdraw and, aided by the advice he has received, will work out his own decisions alone and within himself.

If a non-Indian should suddenly leave his home and go visit an aunt or uncle for a couple of weeks without explaining why he had come and simply sit around by himself not saying much or going out, such behavior would be regarded as unusual. When an Indian does this, however, it is regarded as perfectly normal by his people. No one questions him as to why he came or about what is on his mind. Everyone knows that he has a problem of some kind and is working it out by himself. This is the more typical Indian manner of solving personal problems and the only help the individual has are the stimuli he has received from advice sought recently or in the past.

In a counseling situation, then, the more traditional an Indian is, the less inclined he will be to verbalize and the more he will expect to be "talked to." The "talking to," however, must have no hint of coercion, but rather it should be an offering of some ideas that might be helpful in arriving at a decision. Although the "talking to" (gently and quietly) may not seem to be registering on the Indian client at all, one may be assured that, if the alternatives are suggested in sincerity and not out of a sense of doing a job, every word is registering for future consideration.

Analyzing the psychological aspects of the Indian value of individual freedom, one can see that, when used in its pristine manner, it offers the best possible climate for motivation and human growth. A person lives in an ideal climate for growth when he is aware that he is always free to make his own decisions, is protected by a fence of good advice, and is forgiven even for the most serious mistakes. In this way, he competes with himself instead of with others. Since he makes his own decisions, he is more strongly motivated to attain a given goal because he has only himself to rely on for failure or success. The focus is on a person answering to himself and to self-imposed goals and not to goals and expectations imposed by others so that he is removed from the fear of letting others down. While letting himself down is actually more painful, it is made easier to take because it is less public. Thus it is that a person removed from public expectations and in the privacy of his own mind and secret ambitions, is more truly free and at the same time is more strongly motivated to meaningful goals because they are self-imposed.

For example, a young man who had been a quiet, good-natured boy during his school years, had just graduated from high school. The school principal was congratulating the mother on having such a fine son who had been popular with students and faculty alike and had made a fine record for himself. The mother beamed proudly and said, "Ever since he was a little boy I raised him just like an egg," and she held out her hand as though she were carefully holding an egg. "I never made him do anything he didn't want to do. I always gave him good advice and he learned to listen real good."

In conclusion, then, an Indian is aware of the fact that he must make his own decisions. The more he sees that the alternatives offered are meant for his own good and are non-coercive, the more he will be inclined to decide that which is best for him. The more he feels that he is being pushed into a decision, the less inclined he will be to go in that direction.

Bravery

On being asked the question, "Before the coming of the white man, what was the greatest thing an Indian could do?", elderly Indians may respond: "To strike an enemy; to get lots of eagle feathers; to be a war chief." Although the answers may vary, there is a common element of bravery, as may be seen in the following descriptions.

Among the Indians, when a skirmish was being organized, a great warrior might show up armed only with a coup stick. Indian warfare was frequently the occasion for individual acts of bravery and did not consist necessarily in overwhelming and capturing the enemy but rather in the sum total of brave acts done that day. It was relatively easy to lie in ambush and kill an enemy. It was almost infinitely harder for a warrior to rush under fire toward a number of the enemy, dash in close enough to strike one of them with a small willow stick, then race back toward his own lines with the enemy firing at his back. Thus, a warrior showing up with only a coup stick indicated that he had chosen to battle in the hardest possible way that day.

Whenever one did a notably brave deed, he was awarded an eagle feather, which carried prestige similar to the Congressional Medal of Honor today. The warrior could wear the feather in his hair or on his lance or attach it to his dwelling. When he had received many eagle feathers, he could then make them into a warbonnet. A warbonnet, then, was an impressive symbol of many brave deeds. If more brave

If that is indeed true of the Dacota, it cannot be extended to "all Indians". The Iroquoians rated, probably in this order:

(or the orator first)
1. The wise Councillor (man or woman)
2. The eloquent orator in Council
3. The clever war strategist (Captain)
4. The brave individual warrior

deeds were performed, these feathers could hang on a long tail from the warbonnet.

The act of being a war chief was admired because the very title implied that this particular man was the bravest of all. When a young man was old enough to fight, he did not gather his friends and organize a raid; he first had to prove himself. On being invited into a warrior society, he started at the bottom by tending the horses and doing other menial chores for the conduct of a raid until he had learned the ropes. A series of brave deeds moved him up the ladder. Only when he had really established himself as an outstanding, brave warrior would others come to him and ask him to lead them on a raid. Being a war chief, then, meant that a person had earned the position by many brave deeds.

The bravery in a man was not admired for acts done only when he went on the warpath. These brave acts were relatively infrequent compared to the other, more constant area for the exercise of bravery, the very act of providing for his family. Once a hunting party set foot outside the village circle, the others never knew for sure whether they would see them alive again. They were in constant danger from the animals they hunted and from enemies. Thus, a man had supreme status as a man because he literally risked his life to support his family.

The Indian was conditioned not to show fear in the face of danger or threat. The children learned this behavior early from those around them. If a child began to whimper from fear on seeing his father leave for the hunt, he would hear the familiar "Ssshhh . . ." from the mother and would look into the usually sympathetic face to see, in this circumstance, a face showing no emotion. A child soon learned to face threatening situations without *showing* any fear. To this day, Indians face threatening situations with impassive faces that can belie fearful emotions within. As an eighth-grade Indian boy once said, "We don't make a face." In non-threatening situations where external emotional response is expected the Indian is like anyone else. It is in strange or threatening situations that he will *show* no fear until the situation is evaluated. Bravery is the act of facing a hard thing without showing fear or running from it. In order to have true bravery, fear must be present. It is the overcoming of the fear that makes the act of bravery admirable.

If schools offered Indian cultural courses, young people could be made aware of historical and psychological forces that have shaped their current thinking and behavior and old values could receive new applications. For example, in regard to the value of bravery they could be made to see that it is exercised not in facing unusual dangers but in carrying out daily obligations.

3

Indian Personality

It is generally recognized that culture is one of the main determinants of personality (Barnouw, 1963; Spiro, 1959). People from the same culture, learning common responses to their environment, will develop similar psychological characteristics. It is the unique organization of these psychological characteristics in interaction with the environment that makes each personality different among people of the same culture. Among the individuals making up a culture, however, there is sufficient overlapping and similarity of traits to identify a common personality structure.

The manner in which we react to objects, people, and situations depends partially upon our original experiences with them and, more largely, upon how we are taught to react to them. This is to say that our perceptions, the meanings we impose upon objects, people, and situations, are largely learned and they are learned from our group. Recalling that no consistent behavior is arrived at randomly or haphazardly but adaptively, and recalling that the Indian people have worked out, through many centuries of testing, perceptions of God, themselves, their fellow man, and the universe, it follows that young Indian people learning their perceptions of and their reactions to these four principal areas of concern will develop common personality characteristics that will be peculiarly Indian.

From knowledge of the Indian values already outlined, it will be easier to understand the forces shaping a "common" Indian personality. This is not to say that each and every Indian will have each and every one of the following characteristics but that within the population the majority will exhibit most of them in varying degrees. Also, this is not to say that each and every Indian characteristic will be different from each and every characteristic of other cultures. There will be similarities and overlapping but the forces shaping each side will be different.

Deriving from the Indian value of adjustment to or harmony with nature, one of the most obvious and pervading characteristics of the Indian personality is that of wanting to get along with people. His desire to get along, especially with his own group, is so strong that to point out that his group expects something of him is frequently the best way of motivating him to a desirable course of action.

The human part of the Indian's environment has two areas, the non-Indian and the Indian. In his built-in mental set to get along with everyone, the Indian has no problem in exercising this value with the Indian group. But he receives a severe jolt when he tries to exercise it with the non-Indian or white group because he perceives this group as not approving of him. The modern Indian does want to plan for tomorrow and does want to support his family at a level that he chooses, but he wants to do so without the all-consuming drive for upward social mobility. For this reason, a pervading characteristic of the Indian's personality is one of uneasiness as he is thrust more and more into the non-Indian world. Typically, as an Indian in a threatening situation, he hides this uneasiness with an impassive face.

The Indian is probably not aware that his ability to face hardships has created almost a stereotype of this facet of his personality among non-Indians. This is indicated by such common phrases as "Indian stoicism," "he took it like an Indian," or, in instances of dangerous patrols in the armed forces, "Get the 'chief'; he will go." Deriving from historical instances in which bravery was a way of life and also more recently from a life of hardship on reservations, the Indian can face and accept difficulties and disappointments better than his white counterpart. Life for everyone is made up of a series of disappointments and the calm manner in which an Indian can meet his disappointments is an advantageous trait of the Indian personality. The stereotype of the unemotional Indian makes some people think that the reason Indians do not show more emotion is that they do not feel as deeply as other people. It must be recalled that it is only in the face of threatening situations that the Indian conceals feelings of fear and that in situations calling for other responses, for example, joy or sadness, his behavior is as "normal" as anyone else's.

Urbanized man is becoming increasingly aware that he must return to nature for his own renewal. The more that technology, whether in his work or in his manner of living, dominates him and the more that buildings and asphalt cut him off from nature, the less human man becomes. The Indian has this "constant renewal" relationship to nature built into his very soul. The Indian can rearrange and use nature without losing his reverence for it. Like many of their youthful white counterparts who are becoming increasingly alienated from the denominations of their fathers, educated young Indian people are becoming disenchanted with the structure and impersonal, institutionalized features of Christianity. While alienated young white people are searching for new ways to respond to God, the young Indian people have their old ways to fall back upon and are increasingly discovering and revitalizing them. Many ingeniously manage to keep the essence of a personal Christianity and, while filtering out the undesirable institutional features, merge their personal or "gospel" Christianity with their old religions. This important religious facet of the Indian personality emerges more and more with maturity.

Aptly called the "Modern Indian," the "successful" Indian emerges with the following personality characteristics which he has managed to maintain despite the unwitting efforts of the schools to suppress them. This type, appearing more and more in the persons of Indian college graduates and of established members of the communities, can well serve as a model for the young Indian people currently striving to survive the average school system.

The modern Indian combines his marvelous manner of getting along with others with his competitiveness for the group instead of just for himself.

The modern Indian combines his admirable ability to enjoy the "now" with intelligent planning and preparation for tomorrow.

The modern Indian conquers and uses nature (cars, electricity, etc.) without losing his "constant renewal" contact with and his reverence for nature.

The modern Indian combines his desire to achieve and to do his best with his ability to take disappointments calmly.

The modern Indian has the ability to choose freely, to achieve the level at which he wants to live (skilled labor, professional) and to be content in it without driving for status or unnecessary material possessions.

The modern Indian retains his constant awareness of God as part of his life amid the distraction of the modern world; not measuring his fellow man by money but by his intrinsic worth, he feels more comfortable with himself and the world.

Built upon his Indian values, the modern Indian personality is not only viable but instructive and enriching. These qualities of personality can be encouraged by his school environment.

Indian Motivation

Many a non-Indian visitor has come to a reservation, seen the poor living conditions within sight and sound of modern highways and high-speed cars and asked, "How do you motivate these people?" What they are really saying is, "How do you make them want what we want?" Many a teacher or counselor of Indian students, discouraged at the apparent lack of response, will ask, "How do you motivate these kids?" Again, what they are really saying is "How do we make these kids want what we want for them?"

Whether one defines a motive as "an expectancy of pleasantness or unpleasantness" (McKeachie, 1966) or "as the tendency to strive for goals" (Tolman, 1951) or as "an event which arouses the organism" (Hebb, 1955), the expectancy, the tendency or the event, are all stimuli to something wanted. We are moved, in the sense of being motivated, then, by our wants. If one wonders how to motivate a person, he must answer the question, "What does he want?" If one can supply a person's wants, he will move him or motivate him.

To answer the question, then, as to what will motivate an Indian is to ask, "What does the Indian want?" The Indian, as a human being, has the same wants that any other human being has: self-acceptance, acceptance from others, and self-fulfillment. These wants are sometimes called the "triple goal" which is intrinsic to human nature and common to all men in all cultures. The acts that one will select to gain self-acceptance, acceptance from others, and self-fulfillment will be those which he learns in his culture. These acts, in turn, become learned needs (act needs) intrinsically connected to and leading to models of human success as perceived by a given culture. The triple goal, then, is common to all men, but the acts leading to the triple goal will be learned acts or culturally-induced acts. Whereas all men will share the triple goal, they will not necessarily share agreement as to what acts lead to the triple goal because these acts are intrinsically connected to models of human success as perceived by a given culture. Acts conducive to the triple goal for a Ubangi are not necessarily the acts that a Wall Street banker would choose, because each has different notions, culturally-induced, as to what constitutes a successful person.

An Indian, then, wants the same triple goal — self-acceptance, acceptance from others and self-fulfillment — that everyone else wants. The acts leading to this triple goal will not necessarily be those selected by the white man because the Indian does not have the same notion of human success to which these acts are intrinsically connected. If a school wants to motivate an Indian, then, it must create conditions in which he can achieve self-acceptance, acceptance from others, and self-fulfillment. In so doing, it must set up conditions in which he can pursue models of Indian human success and pursue these models with culturally induced acts (value acts) intrinsically connected to such models.

A person first learns to accept himself by perceiving that his primary group, his family, accepts him. As he moves from his family group into larger community groups this initial experience of being accepted must be continually reinforced by the larger groups (community, school) that surround his family. Interruptions to this need for constant reinforcement by accepting experiences will arrest his concomitant experience of self-acceptance and cause blocks in his growth as a person. As the Indian child moves from his family group into his community group he experiences the community group reinforcing his initial experiences of acceptance by his family. As his world expands and he moves from his family and community into larger concentric groups, the next group that he meets is in the school. It is in this new, largest, and power-positioned group that he meets his first interruption in being accepted.

As his parents take him into this new community, he does not get the same kind of joyful, anticipatory cues from them that he would get if they were taking him to an Indian event, such as a meeting, feast or rodeo. Instead, the parents are more subdued and unconsciously emit a "this-is-something-we-have-to-do" attitude. As he moves for the first time into the white world, unconscious fears and doubts about being accepted begin to rise.

The first formal learning experience that the Indian child should have as he moves into this new, larger world of the school community should be an extension of his previous experiences. This would be the next logical step for his development as a person; the new, larger community would be reinforcing his earlier experiences of being accepted as he moved from his Indian family into his Indian community. Instead, the reader "Dick and Jane" is put into his hands, the first obstacle to his development is placed, and his troubles begin. Although the child cannot verbalize it at the time, it gradually dawns upon him that the larger, all enveloping white world into which he is moving does not approve of his Indian group.

Because the school has not set up conditions in which the child can experience his Indian group as being accepted by the larger group, by the time the counselor gets what is left of the Indian student population still in school, his work with the Indian students is largely therapeutic. The counselor, therefore, has to start where the school should have started nine or ten years ago. He has to set up seminars, group sessions, or classes in which Indian students can be made aware of their values, culture, and history, because no one can be proud of himself unless he is proud of his group. One lecture or one seminar or even one course is not enough because it is impossible to overcome in a few months the negative habits of thought that have been built up and have become functional over a number of years. Seeds can be planted for future fruition, however, because human growth is dynamic; even though stunted for a while, growth will resume if the obstacles are removed.

From time to time, attitudinal inventories are taken of Indian students in order to find out to what degree they are still Indian in their way of thinking and/or how much of the white values they have assimilated. Most of these studies show that the longer an Indian student stays in school, the more he will verbalize white values. At this point, some people quickly and erroneously conclude that this or that school system is working and that these students are finally "swinging over." The implication is often drawn that such Indian students are finally being motivated by the values of the dominant culture and that they have given up much of their Indian way of thinking. The main difficulty with such conclusions is that what the Indian students put down on paper is more often than not belied by their subsequent behavior. No matter how similar the expressed attitudes may appear to those of white students after such testing, they still back off from the white world and do not reflect its attitudes in their conduct.

One explanation for this phenomenon is that, while the Indian students see and want the good things of the white world, they still hesitate when they perceive the non-acceptance that they would have to endure in order to gain them. They would rather forego them than compromise their Indian values. Another explanation is that from the time the Indian youngster enters school and learns how to march down the hall with his classmates in single file, sit in a given place and hand back on paper what the teacher puts on the board, he learns to adapt to the stimuli of the school culture by exhibiting the responses expected of him and overtly, he appears to have internalized expected behavior. But the Indian child will not be effectively motivated until the schools set up conditions from the first grade upward, in which he is made aware of his values (the acts culturally important to him for the triple goal) and taught how to utilize these values in the modern world.

In summary, an Indian is motivated towards his goals of self-acceptance, acceptance from others and self-fulfillment by pride in his values which stimulate him to be able to face hard things without showing fear or running from them, to get along with others, including non-Indians, to choose freely the level at which he wants to live and to provide for his family at that level, to compete for and support his group, to accept others for what they are and not for what they have, and to be constantly aware of God in the nature that he reveres as one, holy and related.

4

Conflicts with Values of the Dominant Culture

Since the Indian also lives in the white man's world, it is necessary to review briefly some aspects of the value system of the dominant culture in order to identify areas of positive and negative interaction. Among social scientists describing American values, the writer regards the work of Williams (1960) among the best available and gratefully acknowledges his research. In abbreviated form, the major American values are described under the following headings:

Material achievement and money success

Deriving from the Protestant ethic, this value finds its expression in Horatio Alger as its mythical hero, the poor boy who, by hard work, rose to great wealth. Clean living, virtue, and hard work will be rewarded by material success. For this reason, in the dominant culture a man is judged by his possessions or by what he has and, if he has many possessions of great material value, he is regarded as a success. We have seen that Indian people judge people by what they are within. If a person does not measure up as generous and filled with Indian wisdom, then the secondary attributes, his possessions, do not impress them.

Activity and work

In the beginning of American culture, activity and work were the means to the primary value of material achievement and monetary success. Activity and work became so much a part of American life, however, that it became more of an end in itself than a means. "Keep busy" or "Let's do something" are prevailing attitudes. Even in recreation, people exhaust themselves in furious activities over weekends and vacations on the assumption that the more they cram in, the more they do, the more they enjoy themselves. This attitude leaves little time for talking, visiting, and contemplating nature which are so highly regarded among the Indians.

Morality

Many people in the dominant culture will say what others should do in terms of right or wrong but their own actions belie their words. The recent protests of young people from hippies to college dissidents are a reaction to this double standard. Indian people have many broken treaties to testify to the white man's tendency to sacrifice principle to expediency.

Humanitarian attitude

There is a strong inclination in most of the people of the dominant culture to help the underdog or those who are less fortunate. This attitude is kindly but operates within limits. The less fortunate are offered various forms of help until they become an economic threat to those above them in the socio-economic ladder. Within these limits, Americans are quick to solicit collections to help people in need. It is apparent that this value is very similar to the Indian value of sharing and generosity, except that among the Indians the attitude of helping others does not have the limitations for its exercise that it has among the whites. It is, however, a value similarity that should be stressed in order to develop as many ties as possible between the two cultures.

Efficiency and practicality

In the white culture, efficient and practical knowledge ordered toward making money or organizing things and people to turn out more products is greatly admired. Businessmen who know how to run huge companies with thousands of people working in them are greater heroes than teachers and college professors and are rewarded accordingly.

Progress

Sometimes called "linear progress", the idea in this value is that progress consists of the constant improvement of things under the assumption that by making things better, people in some manner are improved and made better. While the dominant culture is oriented to and absorbed in the future, rendering many people incapable of really enjoying the "now", the Indian focuses on the "now" and truly enjoys it. True progress to the Indian mind is progress in or improvement of human relations.

Material comfort

Material comforts are valued not only for making life easier but often as status symbols. What begin as luxury items soon become necessities. Many develop obsessions for acquiring the latest gadgets and appliances with the result that material comforts become virtually an end in themselves. Indian people enjoy material comforts as much as others but manage to avoid making them ends in themselves or acquiring them at the expense of good human relations.

Equality

The value of equality holds that all men are created equal and should have equal opportunities. This belief is widely shared. It is a belief that no matter where the person's initial position on the socio-economic ladder, if he works hard enough he can "go to the top."

Freedom

This value implies that everyone is free to do what he wants within the limits of the law. This country began with this new ideal of freedom but as it built up and became more complicated and socially stratified, it soon became apparent that the poorer a person was the less free he was. In the Indian system, a person, by reason of the value of individual freedom, is more truly free because his freedom is not restricted by reason of poverty or age. Even Indian children enjoy this value of individual freedom.

External conformity

Although it is widely believed that a person can be an individual and be different, as soon as an individual or a group of individuals are different the majority of the people immediately clamor for conformity. This American value does not cause any particular kind of conflict among the Indian people because they too have their desires and norms of Indian conformity. In the Indian system, however, if a person wants to be different he is less criticized by reason of the value of individual freedom and there is less pressure from the majority group to force him into line.

Science

Sometimes called scientific rationalism, this value places supreme importance on mathematics, chemistry, physics, and biology as the means for conquering nature. There is a widely-held belief that given the time and money science, by conquering nature, will solve everything. But the restricting of certitude only to knowledge gained from manipulable variables that can be physically measured may often lead to the forgetting of man and his human values.

Nationalism and patriotism

The average citizen of any country is patriotic, thinks his country's way of life is the best in the world, and will defend it when threatened. The Indian people share this civic virtue with other Americans but the Indian is more aware of defending the land along with his way of life because the two are so mystically one to him.

Democracy

The belief that the common man should have a choice in deciding who is going to represent him in government and that the same common man will make intelligent choices is one of the basic values of this country. This value is founded on the belief that every individual has dignity and should have the opportunity for maximum fulfillment with a minimum of government restriction. Again, here is a value that the Indian shares strongly with the white. Long before the coming of the Europeans, many Indian peoples were practicing forms of democracy unheard of in Europe.

Punished Responses

The outside world of white America constantly impinges on the Indian's mind, often causing severe conflicts arising from a foreign system of values. Expected behaviors, contrary to certain Indian behaviors, are all the more threatening because the white is in the power position. This fact cannot be over-emphasized. One ordinarily moves away from people whose behavior and expectations upset him. The Indian cannot do this in regard to the white and the white's power position makes the Indian feel that he is truly trapped in the worst possible way.

Certain research findings in animal learning have been successfully applied to human behavior. From such research the terms "rewarded response" and "punished response" have become almost commonplace in the language. Desired behaviors can be developed by rewarding the desired response and undesirable behaviors can be extinguished by not rewarding or by punishing the undesired response. A rat, for instance, soon learns how to open a door if, in doing so, he enjoys a reward in the form of food. The way to extinguish this learned response is to stop rewarding the response or to punish the response. Hence, a rat who formerly opened a door and was rewarded with food, stops opening the door when, instead of being greeted with food, he is greeted with an electric shock. He backs off from his former behavior because he is now punished.

The Indian in his own world receives a rewarded response in excercising behavior learned from his values. But when he tries to apply that behavior to the outside world, he gets a punished response. The tragedy is that both sides, for the most part, are expressing their values at an unconscious level with the result that the Indian is not aware of why is he being punished and the white is not aware that he is punishing the Indian.

When an Indian had to hunt to support his family, he was rewarded with his society's perception of him as a supreme man and reinforced in his self-esteem. The fact that the hunt was an occasional activity did not derogate from his recognition because when he did engage in it he showed great bravery. Consequently, long after the historical conditions in which it developed had passed, the attitude towards work has been that it is something undertaken periodically to satisfy immediate needs. White employers who have had experience with Indians working for a while and quitting will tell subsequent Indian applicants that they do not hire Indians because they are unreliable or undependable. The white is unconsciously exercising the daily, eight-to-five, ethic of industriousness and the Indian is unconsciously expressing the traditional attitude developed in the situation when work was of a very intense but seasonal nature. In exercising an expected Indian behavior the Indian receives a punished response.

The value of sharing and generosity in the old days meant that one lived and acted as a "group individual." What one acquired the whole group acquired and shared. Things were acquired in order to give and in this way a person found acceptance by others. Security was found not in the confidence that the individual would somehow find a way but in the knowledge that the group would function as a unit to provide what was needed. In essence, this value meant that people had a right to one another's shareable possessions when they needed them.

One was expected to share. Today, when Indian people share with one another, the punishing response that they get from the white culture is to be told that they are wasteful and prodigal. The white, expressing the value of planning by acquiring personal property, tells the Indian that he is wasteful in immediately using up his goods by sharing them.

The Indian, perceiving himself as a part of the whole of nature, endeavors to adjust himself to it. Since people are the most important segment of total nature, the priorities in the Indian's mind are people first, things second. He adjusts himself to people by trying to get along with them, since he perceives himself as related to all. He adjusts inanimate nature to himself just enough to get along. The Indian can set his own achievement level and is not beset by a compulsive drive towards unlimited upward social mobility. He has a unique ability to focus on the present and to enjoy the "now" in people. For this attitude, the criticism the Indian gets from the dominant culture (the punishing response) is to be told that he does not try to improve himself. Because the Indian does not have an all-absorbing focus on tomorrow and typically does not show obvious physical improvements around his house indicating "progress", he is told that he has no "drive", does not want to "get ahead", and is without ambition.

No matter how much the Indian consciously or unconsciously perceives that the dominant culture is wrong in expecting non-Indian behavior from the Indian, the aggravations provoked in the Indian are profoundly disturbing because the white is in the power position. If one should imagine himself as forced to live among another people whose whole way of life was diametrically and jarringly opposed to his own and that his whole survival as a person depended upon some kind of accommodation to those in the power position, he would come a little closer to realizing the apprehension of an Indian toward the dominant culture. A resolution of these conflicts may be made by showing both sides the psycho-socio-historical sources of these behaviors and by bringing these attitudes to a point of awareness so that by conscious choices the values may generate more appropriate behavior.

Negative Influences

In order to understand one's behavior adequately, the principal remote and proximate forces that act upon it must be taken into account. The remote forces shaping one's behavior are the psycho-socio-historical forces in his culture that have transpired to shape attitudes before he was born. These attitudes, in the minds of his parents and grandparents, begin to shape one from the moment he is born. In very brief outline, we have seen these remote forces in the short description of the Indian value system.

We shall now consider some of the principal forces shaping Indian behavior that begin working on him from the time he is a fetus. Until a few years ago, it was thought that in order to understand a person's behavior, one could go back no further than to the moment of birth. Due to fairly recent experiments, however, it is now known that the human organism begins to learn, not at the moment of birth, but while it is still a fetus. At about four to five months of age, a mild shock near the human womb, followed by a noise, can cause the fetus to respond by twitching or moving. After pairing these stimuli for a while, the noise alone can be used and the fetus will respond by moving.

When one studies the first forces shaping Indian behavior at this starting point, one can see that life is begun in the best of all possible environments — a womb existence in which everything is peaceful, calm, totally accepting, and free of tensions. For there is no human being more peaceful and serene than the traditional Indian wife expecting a baby. Deriving from the Indian value of adjustment to nature, having children is the highest form of female fulfillment and the traditional Indian mother is a picture of total contentment. This peaceful condition of the mother, in turn, causes an ideal womb climate in which everything is accepting, peaceful, and free of tension. The Indian fetus' first experience of reality, then, is a world in which he initiates activity and in which the environment is totally accepting and ideal. From the moment he is born, the Indian baby continues to initiate actions which are received in a totally permissive environment. He gets anything he wants. When he cries he is immediately comforted by feeding, changing, or coddling. The world that he knows first is his Indian world in which he is made to feel important because he gets anything he wants.

The day soon comes, however, when the child is made aware of another world outside his Indian world, and the knowledge of this non-Indian world first comes as a frightening threat to his autonomy and self-worth. It is the day that his mother, unconsciously transmitting her own fears of the non-Indian world, in an attempt to frighten him into silence, holds him close and says, *Ssshhh . . . wasicu anigni kte,* "If you don't be quiet, a white man will get you and take you home." It is now well established that first impressions remain at least in the subconscious. The Indian child's first impression of the non-Indian world is that it is threatening and hostile to him. Most children grow up to discover that the "bogey man" their mother threatened them with is a phantom of the imagination and does not exist. The Indian child, however, as he grows up can look out the window and see the "bogey man" going down the road in his pickup truck. The white man might look all right and even appear friendly, but the Indian child has already perceived him as threatening and hostile. For most it will remain that way the rest of their lives. As the Indian child grows, he will meet individual whites whom he will like and will accept. These positive experiences, however, do not always change the threatening complexion of his perceptions of whites. In order to maintain cognitive consistency, he tells himself that those accepted individuals are exceptions. The general area of the white world still remains threatening.

When the Indian child starts to school, he meets many non-Indians whom he accepts, for example, certain teachers, janitors, perhaps even the principal, with the result that this conscious fear goes "underground" or is repressed for a few years. After the first two or three years required to become adjusted to the school culture, many Indian children enjoy an additional two to three years of successful achievement. Thus, during the fourth, fifth, and sixth grades, depending on the area of the country, they often perform well in school.

At adolescence, however, or beginning around the seventh-grade level, several things happen which bring to the surface the Indian child's original, fearful impression of whites. It is during this pre-adult stage that he begins to want to make his mark and, most basically, to achieve that which everyone wants — acceptance of himself from others. As a small child, he expected the acceptance and the pat on the head because this was the right of all children *as* children. Now, however, he begins to want acceptance as a worthy person in his own right. As he looks around him, it dawns upon him that in order to make a decent living for his future family, he must eventually leave his Indian home and go into the non-Indian world to learn the necessary skills. It also dawns upon him for the first time that the norms by which the dominant culture judge a worthy person are those of material achievement. For the first time he becomes aware that many members of the dominant culture live in a better and more expensive house, wear better and more expensive clothes, and drive shiny new cars. He begins to believe that he does not measure up to their norms. Since he does not measure up to their norms, he perceives that they reject him as a person. Yet, it is into and among these non-accepting people that he must eventually move in order to support his family. Ordinarily, when one perceives disapproval from a group, he simply moves away from it. The fact that the white is in the power position even on the reservation effectively puts the Indian at his mercy and creates a classical situation of frustration in which he can neither fight nor flee. On the one hand, the Indian wants to learn how to make a decent living for his family. On the other hand, he feels that he can not make himself go among people who disapprove of him as a person. The closer the Indian student gets to the time when he must go out (graduation), the more likely he will be to back off and refuse to go.

It is during this pre-adolescent and adolescent period that the Indian child not only perceives non-acceptance because he does not measure up to outside norms of human success, but also because he is an Indian. He slowly learns with growing dismay that the outside group expects all Indians, including him, to be no good, undependable, lazy, and to get drunk every chance they get. Although he first meets this awareness with disbelief, it slowly and insidiously begins to influence his thinking so that eventually he begins to view himself in this way. His original perception of himself as someone worthy begins to break down and he gradually begins to act the way those in the power position expect him to act, that is, "no good." Other Indians who have already succumbed to this perceived negative image of themselves reinforce this newly expected set of behaviors by telling the younger Indian, "Come on. We're supposed to get drunk. We're Indians." On recovering from a binge, again and again a young Indian person responding to a school official or to a counselor as to what happened will hang his head and simply say, "I'm just no good." The tragedy is that so many really believe it.

The trouble all began back in the first grade at the moment the school put the "Dick and Jane" type of reader into his hands. Usually, instead of following the basic pedagogical principle of beginning with the child where he is, the teacher began with the Indian boy and girl as though they were Dick and Jane in the suburbs with the huge green lawn, shiny car in the driveway, Daddy in a business suit, Mother trim and stylish, and almost every page suggesting affluence and filled with smiling white faces reflecting the good life of their world.

What do such stories as "My First Ride on an Elevator," or "I Visit the Fire Station," mean to an Indian child at Porcupine, South Dakota? From the first grade on, the Indian child is fed a steady intellectual diet of unrelated content subtly loaded with dominant culture values, especially as to what constitutes success as a person. Although the Indian child cannot verbalize it, it slowly dawns upon him that since the school teaches only what is important and necessary to know and that nothing Indian is ever taught him, there must not be anything important in the Indian world. If this is true of the world from which he came and which produced him, he as an Indian must not be very important.

During this time the Indian child may search the text books for some clue to his history and identity and find that, more often than not, they treat him as a non-person (Vogel, 1968) and that when mention is made of the Indian world it is in the context of savages who blocked progress. During the course of his schooling, the white youngster is taught American history and eventually sociology or some type of social psychology so that he is made aware of the psycho-socio-historical forces that shaped his values. With this knowledge he can understand his behavior and can answer the question as to his cultural identity. The Indian youngster is taught nothing of the great psycho-socio-historical forces that shaped his values and therefore cannot proudly answer the question "Who Am I?" By ignoring him, the school is implying that he is inferior and its prestigious position drives home this point. The Indian youngster has no basis for developing an idea of his self-worth. It is after this psychological battering that the secondary school counselor comes in contact with the Indian student — if the student survives that long. To the counselor the school says in effect, "There seems to be something wrong with him. See what you can do about it." But no attempt is made to correct the conditions in which the problem developed.

Research Evidence of Psychological Conflicts

Psychological testing data and clinical evidence are conclusive and uniform in revealing rather severe mental health problems among many Indian adolescents. It is true that most of the mental health concepts and instruments were developed in the white culture, yielding evidence of maladaptive behavior among white youth, but a closer examination of the evidence also reveals indications of Indian maladaptive behavior. Krush and Bjork (1965) in researching mental health problems among children in an Indian boarding school found considerable feelings of rejection by relatives because they were sent to a boarding school. These feelings were accompanied by depression, feelings of isolation, and antisocial behavior toward their own group as well as anxiety and self-recrimination. In further research (1966) on the same population the same investigators concluded that frequency of moving from place to place which was so characteristic of many of the students and the accompanying necessity of conforming to different standards resulted in confusion and personality disorganization. This frequency of movement also blocked the development of lasting relations in which love and concern could enjoy adequate maturation. This "psychosocial nomadism" resulted in inward disturbance.

Saslow and Harrover (1968), researching the psychosocial adjustment of Indian youth in a large Indian boarding school, report that the school experiences of Indian students tend to accentuate rather than resolve their identity problems and result in a subsequent breakdown of an adequate self-image and the competence needed to manifest achieving behavior. Unfortunate school experiences, joined to a reality-based lack of economic opportunity cause the Indian student to develop feelings of limited self-worth, alienation, and helplessness. Patterns of trust and personal worth developed at home before beginning the school experience seem to deteriorate as the Indian student moves through school.

Under a National Institute of Mental Health grant the author tested 415 Indian adolescents and 223 other adolescents utilizing 28 different psychological variables. Six Indian groups were compared with six non-Indian groups and then five other Indian groups were compared with each other. In all of the Indian and non-Indian comparison, the same pattern emerged. At a significant level Indian students revealed themselves as having a higher incidence of feelings of rejection, depression, and anxiety, accompanied by tendencies to withdraw and feelings of social alienation even from their own group. Indian eighth-grade students in comparison with Indian twelfth-grade students showed themselves significantly different in a higher incidence of feelings of powerlessness, rejection, depression, and alienation. Indian dropouts when compared to Indians who stayed in school showed the most marked feelings of rejection, depression, and alienation. The concept of alienation appeared to be central in explaining the behavior of the Indian students. In another study Spilka and Bryde (1965) found that alienation, with its components of powerlessness, normlessness and helplessness, increased as school achievement decreased among 105 Indian high school students from the ninth to eleventh grades. It was not clear from the data whether failure to perform adequately led to feelings of inadequacy and defeat, or whether feelings of inadequacy and defeat deriving from other forces led to poor achievement. It was concluded, however, that the pattern of influences might well be mutually supportive and circular.

The Pine Ridge Community Mental Health Program, funded by the Public Health Service, and unique in its kind, conducts research and develops programs for a comprehensive community mental health program. In a recent report (Maynard, 1969) it is said that the Indian teenager in that area is "beset with feelings of insecurity, alienation, and anxiety . . ." Furthermore, the same young people have "deep feelings of inferiority arising from economic deprivation, inadequate education, and a negative image of Indians." Even more disturbing is the forty-four attempted suicides reported to the Program during the year 1968. Using a gross means of comparison it was estimated that this rate of suicide attempts is five times higher than the national rate. Other reservations also report much higher rates of suicide attempts than the national rate.

The above studies are cited in order to enable the counselor to understand better the severe stress under which his Indian clients will most likely be laboring. Since the school is the main area for the confrontation between the Indian child and the dominant culture, it is in the school that most of these troubles arise. Considering the impeding forces at work in his life, it is a marvelous tribute to the strength of the Indian character that he has stood up under them as well as he has.

Psychological damage will continue until the schools educating Indian children begin with the Indian child where he is. In the first grade, utilizing Dolch's word-list (1943) or whatever list of required words one chooses, the content of the early basic readers for the first three grades should center upon Indian values. These Indian values should be used for establishing early positive identity and, during the following grades, motivation toward goals of human fulfillment acceptable to the Indian people. At the fourth-grade level Indian history should begin, Indian values should be expanded, and mental health concepts should be introduced. Each grade up to twelfth-grade high school should have its Indian textbook with Indian values, culture, and history deepened and expanded. This does not mean that the other required courses such as mathematics and English should be thrown out. Obviously these courses provide needed knowledge for today's world. The Indian course would be the "meat and potatoes" course, the foundation or motivating course for learning the other necessary subjects, as well as the course designed to meet cultural needs. Through such a course of study the Indian student could learn how to function proudly in the pluralistic society in which we all must live.

5

Guidance and the
Indian Student

There is no magic formula or gimmick for successful counseling with Indians. Instead of methods or techniques, one should consider the conditions necessary for functioning successfully as a counselor of Indian students.

The first condition is that the counselor know his Indian client. This means that he knows the student's goals and degrees of motivation and knows the means to assist the student to achieve his goals.

The second condition is that the counselor have a sincere respect and love for his Indian student. If the counselor perceives the Indian student as, for example, an intriguing sociological specimen, the Indian student will be aware of it and it will block the necessary person-to-person relationship.

The third condition for successfully functioning as a counselor of Indian students is that the counselor must set up the circumstances in which the Indian student himself can become aware of his values so that the counselor can use them consciously for motivation. Seminars, group sessions, or formal classes, conducted by the counselor himself or other qualified people on the staff, must be ongoing experiences for the students, because just as it took time to build up the habits of negative thinking about themselves, so it will take time to build up the opposite, positive habits of thought.

During a role-playing exercise in a graduate class in guidance and counseling, the part of a student was taken by a counselor from an Indian school. The member playing the role of the counselor began by asking routine questions which the "student" answered with a "yes" or a "no", then lapsed into complete silence for several minutes. "Well, say something," the instructor finally said. "But I'm playing the part of an Indian student," said the counselor, "and I am just being realistic." As he persisted in his silent behavior, it quickly dawned upon instructor and class alike that the ordinary counseling techniques, relying so heavily upon the verbalization of the counselee directed by the counselor, do not work with many Indian students who do not verbalize like middle class white students.

During the ensuing discussion, the oft-repeated question, "How do you get them to talk?" revealed just how heavily current counseling procedures rely upon verbalization. The assumption is that if they do not talk, how can you help them? With such an attitude, it quickly becomes apparent that one is trying to fit the student to the method. When it is a fact that the student will not fit the method, then the method, not the student, has to be changed. This means that some other method not founded upon verbalization must be used, a method that fits the student, a method in which the student does not have to talk.

From the value of Good Advice from Indian Wisdom, it will be recalled that when the people are in trouble and need advice they go to a wise, old Indian living in their area. This means two things: a) when faced with a problem they go voluntarily to one they trust, and b) they go expecting to listen.

Translated to a school counseling situation, then, this means that when faced with a problem, the Indian student will go voluntarily only to one he trusts because of that person's knowledge and personal interest, and he goes expecting to listen. Changing the method to fit the student, then, this means that the counselor, at least initially, may be required to do more talking than he normally does. As one Indian father explained to a school official, the proper method of dealing with his son was to "Treat him like I do. Talk to him, — softly." After getting all the facts, the counselor should describe alternatives in a way that avoids any hint of pressuring the Indian student, aware that the Indian student will make his own decision.

It often happens that an Indian student will come to a counselor's office, then just sit quietly paging through a magazine and hardly say a word. Afterwards, an inexperienced counselor might wonder, "I wonder why he came?" One with more experience has learned that for an Indian student there can be a fine relationship set up by silence and one that might be called the communication of silence. In cases like this the Indian student is frequently testing the counselor and signalling his approval of him. His very presence, although spent in silence, is a positive act and it is often preliminary to talking to the counselor about a problem he has in mind. A seasoned counselor comes to recognize this and sets up situations where students can come in, page through magazines or other informational literature without being expected to say anything. Knowing that the client will talk in his own good time, the counselor, after a few words of greeting, can go right on with his work, saying something light now and then or tossing the student a book or a pamphlet he might be interested in.

It frequently happens that an Indian student, reluctant to be the sole object of the attention of a counselor, will come in with two or three friends to talk. In this way, he can diffuse the attention of the counselor to the whole group and during the conversation get in the question that he is really interested in. After several sessions like this, the student will often come back alone if he has something to talk about that warrants greater privacy. Some counselors take advantage of this practice by casually inviting five or six students to drop by together to see some item of interest in his office. Word gets around and other groups drop in from time to time, apparently just to visit. In this way, individuals who would not dream of coming alone become acquainted with the counselor and what his office has to offer. It is also during these group visits that the counselor can casually convey a few ideas about problems common to everyone.

Many Indian people do not have marketable skills. Even for those with skills learned in the military or in various vocational training programs employment opportunities on and near reservations are severely limited. Some reservations are beginning to attract industries and these industries have alleviated somewhat the high unemployment rate which is still, on the average, almost forty per cent, or ten times the national average (Richmond, 1969). By the time a counselor begins working with an Indian student in regard to vocational or college choices, he is working with the cream of the crop because 60 per cent of the Indian students have dropped out by then.

In assisting students, the counselor should have all necessary literature from the *Dictionary of Occupational Titles* to several guidance publications. Among this literature, the *Counselor's Guide to Manpower Information* (Bureau of Labor Statistics, Bulletin 1598, Superintendent of Documents) is very helpful. The counselor should also familiarize himself with the offerings of the nearest Bureau of Indian

Affairs Employment Assistance Office which provides a wide variety of vocational choices and the financial assistance to pursue them. Officials from the nearest BIA Employment Assistance Office are always willing to come to a school and talk to the students about their program. State Employment Service offices will also provide information on request on state and national labor opportunities and will also come to the school to talk to students.

For college oriented Indian students, the Bureau of Indian Affairs offers a limited number of grants each year. Because of limited funds in this college grant program, applications should be made as soon as possible. Many states also offer special college scholarships to Indian students and this information will be available from the State Education Office. More detailed information concerning scholarships of this nature may be found in *Scholarships for American Indian Youth* (revised, 1969) available from Publication Service, Haskell Institute, Lawrence, Kansas, 66044. Many tribes, depending upon their resources, also have scholarship programs for their young people and this information is available from the Tribal Office.

The Use of Tests

The use of tests with Indian students is subject to the well documented criticisms which urge caution regarding their value with subcultural groups in America today. Test scores taken with other variables such as personal motivation and observed performances can serve as relatively useful estimates of certain behaviors such as ability, interest and achievement. There have been Indian high school students who scored very high on intelligence tests and college entrance tests and were apparently ideal candidates for college, but who failed to last even a term in the college situation. On the other hand, there have been Indian high school students, whose miserably low intelligence and college entrance examination scores originally caused shudders in admittance officials, but who succeeded in college. Colleges which have had considerable experience with Indian students are becoming more aware that the best criterion for accepting them should not be test results alone but the recommendation of the school counselor, principal, or teacher. Such people usually know, from observed performances in the local school situation and from personal knowledge of the student's goals, whether the student has the intelligence and motivation to succeed in a college situation.

One of the tests that seems to give a fair appraisal of the Indian student is the General Aptitude Test Battery employed by the Employment Security Department. A combination achievement and aptitude test, the GATB also yields a G score that can be taken as an IQ score and which usually correlates highly with other IQ tests the student has taken. Although most colleges do not find much use in results of the GATB, it can serve as a valuable tool for the counselor. The nearest Employment Security Office is always willing to send in people who will administer this test.

The counselor, from his professional training, will be aware of the other aptitude and interest tests that are available and will have his own preferences. Like the IQ and achievement tests, these tests should be used as rough indicators of the interests and aptitudes of Indian students. The author's experiences indicate that the Stanford-Binet, because it is a power test, comes closer to "measuring" the intelligence of Indian students than any of the other individual IQ tests. Like most children, Indian students tested on the Binet tend to score 10 to 20 points higher than they will on group, timed tests. For this reason, it would be helpful for the Indian student to have someone on the staff who is qualified to give the Binet and Wechsler tests.

The Counselor as Seen by the Indian Student

In the course of writing this monograph, the author called together a group of Indian college students who were enrolled at his home institution in order to learn their perceptions of the role of a counselor. These young Indian people had survived high school and were successfully coping with college. They were close enough to their high school days to remember them vividly and by now were experienced and articulate enough to express these memories clearly and forcefully. It was thought that these young people would be ideal sources for information as to what they think a counselor should do and what his qualifications should be.

In response to the question "What do you think is the job of the counselor?" the Indian college students responded along the following lines. Some said that his job is simply to help the student in any way possible. More specifically, he should be able to inform the students about vocational choices as well as the various college choices available and be able to give the advantages and disadvantages of the various colleges that they could go to. Furthermore, they felt that his job also requires him to be able to help in any way possible with personal problems.

They all agreed that the counselor has an obligation to see all the students in order to impart this information and also in order to inquire about personal problems. In order to fulfill this obligation, they felt that the counselor should set up a schedule of appointments by which he could see everyone at least twice a year in his office. They also felt that it is part of his job to find out how Indian students feel about such things as sex, drinking, teachers, and family problems and they said this with the clear implication that Indians have their own way of looking at these problems. It is the Indian point of view that the counselor should find out about and the best source for this knowledge is from the Indian students themselves and not from the counselor's knowledge of non-Indian students with problems in the same areas.

Many of the students felt that the schools fail in not advertising properly the place and function of the counselor in the school system from the very first days of their junior-high and senior-high school experiences. Since someone has to do this advertising, they felt that this is one of the jobs of the counselor. A number said that they were not aware until it was too late of various course choices they might have made. They pointed out that when an Indian student first comes to school, he thinks that the counselor is just another teacher with a strictly teaching function which includes running to the principal with any unpleasant information he may pick up about the student. Usually a couple of years will elapse before it dawns upon the student that the counselor is not just another teacher but a person with a special function and one to whom he can talk openly about anything without fearing that the counselor will tell anyone. He eventually will get this information through other students, but they felt that it is part of the counselor's job to get this information to the student and to get it across early.

When asked, "What are some of the things that you did not like about your counselors when you were going through high school?", the Indian college students responded eagerly. Most felt that the average counselor had not been close enough to the students. They said this with the clear implication that the students had wanted to be close to someone in the school and the counselor had been the logical one for this position. They did not like the impressions they had gathered that many counselors had seemed too busy with paper work to see them and this had been one factor in preventing this desired closeness. They definitely did not like the appointment system to see a counselor. This, to them, had made for a closed-door system which they blamed on the counselor. As one student said, "You have a problem now that you want help on and you want to talk about it now. You make an appointment and three days later you get in. By then the mood has passed and you don't want to talk about it. This makes the counselor start to pry and you have to make up lies to get out of it." Every one of the other students nodded in agreement.

They definitely did not like having been "dragged in" to the counselor's office because of disciplinary problems. Although they knew that the counselor had not done the "dragging in" they had perceived him as a cooperating part of the system that had subjected them to this unpleasant experience. The questions that the counselor had been invariably compelled to ask in these circumstances, at a time that the student had been too upset to talk about them, had made the experience all the more painful and they had resented the counselor's part in this. They felt that in circumstances like this they should have been given their choice of whether they wanted to see a counselor and then have been given the further choice of selecting their own counselor or a teacher to whom they might have preferred to talk.

Some of the students said they did not like their initial impressions of the counselors as being "big shots" who were too busy to see such insignificant little things as freshmen. Unlike the teachers, who did not have private offices, the counselor had an office all his own which put him right up there with the principal. This office door was always closed and one got in only by the mysterious procedure of making an appointment. They felt that the counselor should have been going to the student, even the lowly freshman, instead of sealed off as someone sacred and inaccessible. From these early impressions they quickly concluded that the counselor was not interested in them and also that since only he and the principal had private offices, then he must have been part of the administration, wielding power and enforcing rules. Again the students blamed the counselor for not having properly oriented them to his function and advertised his job from the very beginning.

Along with this original "big shot" image of the counselor, many of the Indian college students said that they felt too many of the counselors had looked down on them. Such counselors gave the impression of having known all the answers and were only too ready to butt in and give absolute answers without having given the student a chance to explain himself fully. This type of counselor was too quick to make generalizations which the students felt did not apply to their particular problems because the counselor had not heard them out. They resented generalizations for problems which they perceived as narrowly specific. They likewise resented the counselor having given the confident impression that all problems were alike. While they respected the enormous book knowledge that the counselor had, they felt that he drew too much on this knowledge in having arrived at his solutions and not on the knowledge of their problems. They resented having been "snowed" with this knowledge and the counselor having conveyed the impression that "he knew everything." They resented having been interrupted and having had words put in their mouths and they disliked intensely the counselor's habit of having interpreted their actions instead of having let them, under his guidance, come to their own interpretations.

Since many of the Indian college students were by now familiar with basic psychological concepts, they bitterly resented counselors who had hastily applied psychoanalytical concepts to explain some of their behavior while they were in high school. At that time they felt that the application of those heavy-book theories had no pertinence to their problems and now, with a knowledge of those basic concepts, they were, with a touch of bitterness, more sure than ever. Despite their personal rejection of some of the heavy-book theories which were applied to them, many of the Indian college students pointed out that the counselors, after getting all the facts, should be very careful as to what they say because many of the less discriminating students would believe everything they were told and, if the counselor were not absolutely right, he could harm them by not advising them rightly.

Another thing that the Indian college students did not like about many counselors was their attitude about their jobs. They felt that the smiling, eight-to-five interest in the students was merely a professional facade and not a sincere, person-to-person concern that went beyond five o'clock. They felt that with the five o'clock bell the smile was switched off and they were just a lot of names left behind in the office files. Since the counselor was approachable only from eight-to-five and not all the time, they felt that they, on their part, were not being perceived as persons but as just another piece of office business to be fitted into office hours. They felt that their desire for a constant, person-to-person relationship should not have been switched on and off by a clock and they were fully aware that the occurrence of their problems and the corresponding mood to talk about them did not follow a neat schedule.

One of the biggest complaints voiced by all the Indian college students was that the average counselor really does not understand Indian students. Insisting that they are different from non-Indian students, they complained that many counselors never really find out what these differences are. Asked how the counselor could really get to know the Indian students, they quickly said, "Get out there and live with the people." They added that if he could not live among the Indian people for any length of time, he could at least visit in the homes as often as possible and this would give him some idea of the general background from which the students come. If he finds it impossible to visit homes then the next best way to come to understand the Indian people would be to *really* listen with an open mind to the Indian students themselves. When they were asked how long it would take for a new counselor with a sincere, open mind to get a good beginning in understanding the Indian student, they all agreed "about four or five years."

Among the things that the Indian students did not like about some counselors is that during the few times that the counselor sallies forth and mingles among the students he seems to have favorites. They perceived him as being more drawn to those who are lively or who have "good personalities." They complained that this type of counselor does not pay any attention to the "little joe's" or to those who do not respond much. This further alienates the average student who has just as many problems, but because he is not forward like the "lively ones" he does not have the nerve to go to the counselor's office. They thought that the counselor should show strict impartiality and display equal liking for everyone.

The Indian college students were asked, "Just what are some of the main differences between the Indian students and the non-Indian students that the counselor should know about?" At first, they gave the general answer, "Our culture is different and our value system is different in many ways." When asked to be more specific about some of the differences, several pointed out that Indians are not interested, as the white is, in this "social status stuff." They said that they want to make a living, but they do not like the pressure system that makes people want to go up the "social ladder." They just want to "set their own pace" and get along as they choose. Some said that when they are among their own people they are more free and more respected. They said that one of the differences is that they do not like to be pressured and that the white seems to be carried along by pressure from many sides. They want to make their own decisions and would seek help, but not pressure, to make their decisions. In using the phrase "more respected among their own people" they also used the expression "WASP values" and said that they do not go along with these as the way of getting respect from others, and this makes a big difference beween the Indians and whites. They further said that it is annoying that just because Indians are outnumbered, whites should think that this makes their WASP values superior.

Another difference that they pointed out is that the Indian student is a victim of prejudice. This damages him and the counselor should know of this "hurting experience" and how to help the Indian student with it. They also said that too many Indian students have the experience of thinking "no good" about themselves. They said that they hear "You're no good!" even from other Indians, and these remarks, coupled with the prejudice they see around them, just make worse the total experience of feeling "no good." They blamed the schools for this "no good" feeling because the schools do not teach the Indians their heritage and all the good things about the Indian people they should know. Counselors, they said, should be aware of this and know how to cope with it.

They said that another difference is that Indian students have more problems. They pointed out that proportionately there are more broken homes among the Indians and that the counselor should be aware of the home background of each student in order to understand him more fully. Many times a student may miss school because he is needed at home for "family problems" or to help care for the younger children. Also, sometimes his only clothes for school are being washed or he thinks his clothes are not good enough. Many Indian parents are still learning how to live in the white world. This uncertainty in the parents causes, in turn, uncertainty and anxiety in the children. The school should be aware of these reasons and not just condemn the student or get the law on him. The counselor should promote this awareness and relate the concern of the school to help the student to improve his condition by providing opportunities for self-development in an accepting atmosphere.

The Indian college students were asked, "If you were a counselor, how would you get the traditional, reserved, non-verbal type of Indian to talk and relate to you?" They answered that the traditional Indian would communicate verbally and non-verbally in his own fashion if a good relationship is established. The first condition for establishing a good relationship is to show such a person that you *sincerely* like him and are interested in him. This need not be done with much effusion or display of emotion and backslapping. In fact, a quiet approach is the best way to show this interest. Just a quiet, friendly "hello" on meeting in the halls will do for a starter. Through casual conversation, whether in the office or the halls, find out what he is interested in. Show continued interest by giving him an article, a book, or any information pertinent to the subject from time to time without "making a big deal about it." Build upon this to other areas of mutual interest.

According to the students, one of the best ways of building the bridge of good relationships with this traditional type of Indian is to learn his language. They stressed that this learning the language should not be used as a trick, gimmick, or ploy to win his confidence but should be a sincere effort to gain insight into his culture. If the sincerity is there, the student will gratefully perceive it as a sign of interest in his culture and therefore in himself. Even if one foresees that he will never master the language, if he puts aside just ten minutes a day for gathering words and studying them, he will gain both insight into the culture and good relationships with the Indian-language student. It will not be long before this type of student will come to the counselor of his own accord to offer him new or unusual words that he heard from his parents or grandparents. When this happens the student is coming voluntarily and the relationship is established.

Another way of establishing good relationships with this type of student is to ask, whether in the office or recreation room, non-personal questions about Indian life and customs. At first, he may say that he does not know but if he perceives sincerity and persistence he will begin to respond positively. There are certain aspects of private Indian ceremonials that are sacred to the Indian people and these areas should be avoided. Questions concerning public ceremonials are generally acceptable but even here, if one detects evasions, he should quickly move to other topics.

"Use humor," they also said. Light remarks about something serious, a "kind of humorous hinting around," will get a point across while avoiding the jolt of a flat statement or a direct question which can be jarring to the Indian's sense of propriety and privacy. A "gentle teasing" about an acceptable topic will also help to oil the wheels of communication. An invitation offered to two or three together to drop by the office to look at a picture or a book, will help to remove the hesitancy about coming alone and develop the habit of dropping in spontaneously. Also, asking two or three to come in and help with some simple job such as stuffing envelopes or sorting books and papers creates the opportunity to get acquainted. If these experiences can be made pleasant to them, they will begin sticking their heads in the office from time to time inquiring whether you need any help or not.

In the "winding down" conversation following discussion of the specific questions, the Indian college students also made the following spontaneous remarks about the general area of counseling and guidance:

"It's funny," said one of the girls, "now that I look back on it. When I had a problem, I never went to the counselor. I always went to one of my favorite teachers that I could talk to." A number concurred with this remark and said that they did the same thing. All of them agreed that when something was bothering them they always talked it over with their closest friend first; then, if they and their friend could not solve it, they went to a favorite teacher. One of the students, however, said that he and his crowd always went to their counselor because he was a "real buddy" who would "really listen" to them. In summing up this topic they all agreed that the first thing they looked for when they had a problem was not someone with the title or credentials but someone who liked them, understood them, and listened to them.

Now more fully aware of the function of a counselor, several mused that in retrospect, the only time they saw their counselor was once or twice during their junior or senior year and those occasions were just to pick up some test results or get some information on colleges. This led them to repeat what they had said previously about the counselor making his function known to the freshmen as soon as possible. Although they felt that the counselor had the prime responsibility for informing students about the nature of his job, they also felt that if the counselors could get the teachers working with them, the students would get the message much sooner.

One student described his participation in an encounter group, which for him was the most rewarding counseling experience during his high school years. This group was not directed by the official counselor of the school but by one of the teachers with a background in group work. The group began under ideal conditions in that it was not imposed upon them from without; the student and some of his buddies began dropping in after school hours just to "shoot the bull" with the teacher. It was not long before a few more joined the group because it was something to do and also because they found that they could talk to the teacher. As the meetings became regular affairs and as the teacher observed the give and take among the members of the group, he gradually dropped in some encounter group ideas without calling them such or without seeming to impose any rules on the group. After listening to someone divulge a minor confidence that the others had not heard before, he mused aloud how great it was that a person could say something like that and not have it go beyond the group. Although the group had not directly considered it that way before, after a few more remarks to this effect in subsequent meetings they began to impose this collective expectation upon themselves and eventually adopted it as a rule. From exchange of minor confidences, the teacher finally wondered aloud how great it would be if a person could say just anything he wanted, including really big things, and not only would it not go beyond the group, but no matter what was said no one would get sore about it. This sounded like a great idea and the rule, "Don't get sore", was quickly formulated. By inviting comments from as many people as possible concerning someone's gripe, the teacher gradually built up the habit of everyone's chipping in to help solve the problem. Once the group realized that the habit was established, they quickly formulated their own rule to this effect.

It took almost a year before it really dawned upon this student that he could say anything he wanted without anyone getting angry, that he would get group help, and that it would not go beyond the group. It was at this point that the real growth began and has been with him ever since. The student concluded by saying that there was a not too subtle irony in this situation. The school he had attended was under a very strict administration at that time, and since these sessions were after hours, the most meaningful experiences of all his high school years would have been squashed if the administration had known about it.

It was the opinion of the Indian college students that similar sensitivity groups could be successful for Indian students under certain conditions. One condition was that the leader be one whom the students really trusted and respected. Another condition was that he have plenty of patience and not rush things. They also said that the older the students were the better the chances were for success.

The Compleat Counselor of Indian Students

The Indian college students were asked, "If you could have on request your ideal counselor, what are the qualities that you would want in him?" Their answer was as follows:

The ideal counselor for Indian students would be Indian, since no one can talk to an Indian like an Indian. There is instant rapport and no jockeying about for mutual understanding. Even more ideally, there would be a choice between men and women counselors. Although girls prefer to talk to a woman counselor most of the time, there are times when they want to talk to a man counselor. There would also be a sufficient number of counselors, because Indian students have "more problems".

The ideal counselor would be primarily a friend who is always available for help. In order to be this type of friend, the counselor must not be an eight-to-five, professional friend but a constant, open-door friend.

The next quality of the ideal counselor would be that of open-mindedness. An open-minded counselor would really listen to "those kids" and what they are trying to say. Frequently a student may seem to be asking a question when he is not asking a question at all. He is simply trying to tell the counselor how he feels about something. If the counselor were open-minded and without ready answers he would be reading all the signals and getting the real message. For the student, the point of an interview with the counselor is not to get an answer *from* him but to get across *to* him how he feels about something. With true open-mindedness the counselor would be more fully achieving his function as a receiver of messages from students and not a giver of information to them.

The next quality of the ideal counselor would be a thorough knowledge of Indian culture and values. He would not have his own preconceived notions of what an ideal student should be and try to force the Indian student to be that kind of person. By knowing the Indian culture he would know what kind of a person the Indian student would like to be, and would use this knowledge to help the Indian student to that end. Even if the counselor should begin with very little knowledge of Indian culture and values, he would learn this essential body of knowledge by listening to the student as a friend.

The ideal counselor would also be patient. He would be willing to listen to the same problem again and again without showing boredom. No matter how often the student may make the same "goof," the counselor would never show impatience or anger but complete understanding, acceptance and patience. Indians are characteristically much more patient and long-suffering than whites; whites have the reputation among the Indians of having short fuses, low tolerance to frustration, and of blowing up easily. The white counselor must prove to the Indian student that he is an exception to this image, for the Indian will be testing and watching to see whether he is really patient.

Lastly, the ideal counselor would "really know his stuff" as a counselor and know how to use it rightly. The Indian student has a great respect for the enormous knowledge that the counselor has but this knowledge is often wasted if the counselor does not use it judiciously, that is, by really listening first, then using his knowledge to guide the student to what the student wants and not to inject ready answers based on preconceived notions. The counselor's professional knowledge would be largely ineffective unless he develops the preceding qualities to a high degree.

In short, according to the Indian students, the compleat counselor would be a real friend, always there, open-minded, a listener, familiar with them and their culture, always patient with them, and professionally competent. Although simply and briefly stated, this is the work of a lifetime, as anyone in the field knows. And, as a lifetime work of a unique nature, its rewards are the pleasure and joy of a rich and fulfilling life of service.

BIBLIOGRAPHY

Barnouw, V. *Culture and Personality.* Homewood, Illinois: The Dorsey Press, 1963.

Brown, J. (Ed.). *The Sacred Pipe: Black Elk's Account of the Seven Rites of the Oglala Sioux.* Norman, Oklahoma: University of Oklahoma Press, 1953.

Bryde, J. *Modern Indians.* Vermillion, South Dakota: Institute of Indian Studies, 1969.

————. *The Indian Student: A Study of Scholastic Failure and Personality Conflict,* 2nd ed. Vermillion, South Dakota: Institute of Indian Studies, 1970.

Dolch, E. *The Basic Sight Word Test.* Champaign, Illinois: Garrard Publishing Co., 1942.

Hebb, D. "Drives and the CNS," *Psychological Review,* 62:243–254, 1955.

Hickerson, H. *Education for Alienation.* Englewood Cliffs, New Jersey: Prentice-Hall, 1966.

Josephy, A. (Ed.). *The American Heritage Book of Indians.* New York: American Heritage Publishing Co., 1961.

Krush, P. and Bjork, J. "Mental Health Factors in an Indian Boarding School," *Mental Hygiene,* 49: No. 1, 94–103, Jan. 1965.

————. "Some Thoughts on the Formation of Personality Disorder: Study of an Indian Boarding School Population," *American Journal of Psychiatry,* 122: No. 8, Feb., 1966.

Maynard, E. and Twiss, G. *That These People May Live.* Pine Ridge, South Dakota: Community Mental Health Program, U.S. Public Health Service, 1969.

McKeachie, W. and Doyle, C. *Psychology.* Reading, Massachusetts: Addison-Wesley Publishing Co., 1966.

Neihardt, J. *Black Elk Speaks.* Lincoln, Nebraska: University of Nebraska Press, 1961.

Richmond, C. "If you Were Counseling Tom Begay," *Occupational Outlook Quarterly,* U.S. Dept. of Labor, Bureau of Labor Statistics, Vol. 13, No. 1, Spring, 1969.

Saslow, H. and Harrover, M. "Research on Psychosocial Adjustment of Indian Youth," *American Journal of Psychiatry,* 125: No. 2, Aug., 1968.

Spilka, B. and Bryde, J. "Alienation and Achievement among Oglala Sioux Secondary Students," Psychology Department, University of Denver, 1965 (processed).

Spiro, M. "Cultural Heritage, Personal Tensions, and Mental Illness in a South Sea Culture," *Culture and Mental Health,* Opler, M. (Ed.). New York: The Macmillan Co., 1959.

Tolman, E. *Collected Papers in Psychology.* Berkeley: University of California Press, 1951.

Vogel, V. *The Indian in American History.* Chicago: Integrated Education Associates, 1968.

Vontress, C. "Cultural Differences: Implications for Counseling." Paper presented at APGA Convention, Detroit, April 10, 1968. ERIC, ED 023 105, CG 002 494.

Williams, R. *American Society: A Sociological Interpretation,* 2nd ed. New York: Alfred Knopf, 1960.

INDEX